COLLECTION LATOMUS
VOL. 204

THE ROMAN JURISTS AND THE ORGANIZATION OF PRIVATE BUILDING IN THE LATE REPUBLIC AND EARLY EMPIRE

LATOMUS

REVUE D'ÉTUDES LATINES

18, av. Van Cutsem, B. 7500 Tournai

La revue **Latomus**, fondée en 1937 par M.-A. **Kugener**, L. **Herrmann** et M. **Renard** et dirigée actuellement par M. Marcel RENARD, publie des articles, des variétés et discussions, des notes de lecture, des comptes rendus, des notices bibliographiques, des informations pédagogiques ayant trait à tous les domaines de la latinité : textes, littérature, histoire, institutions, archéologie, épigraphie, paléographie, humanisme latin, etc.

Les quelque **1000 pages** qu'elle comporte annuellement contiennent une riche documentation, souvent **inédite** et abondamment **illustrée**.

Montant de l'abonnement au tome XLVIII (1989) :

Prix pour la Belgique :	2.460 FB, port et TVA compris.
Prix pour l'étranger :	2.600 FB, port compris.

Prix des tomes publiés avant l'année en cours :

– pour la Belgique :	2.990 FB, port et TVA compris,
– pour l'étranger :	3.100 FB, port compris.

Les quatre fascicules d'un tome ne sont pas vendus séparément.

C.C.P. **000-0752646-23** de la **Société d'études latines de Bruxelles.**

Une réduction de 20% est accordée aux professeurs de l'enseignement secondaire et de l'enseignement supérieur, aux chercheurs qui font partie d'organismes comme le F.N.R.S., aux étudiants.

Pour l'achat des tomes I à XXI, s'adresser à la Johnson Reprint Corporation, 111, Fifth Avenue, New York 3, New York.

Correspondants :

ESPAGNE : J.-M. BLÁZQUEZ, Instituto de Arqueologia, 4, Duque de Medinaceli, E.-Madrid 14.

ÉTATS-UNIS ET CANADA : Prof. Allen M. WARD, Dept. of History, Box U-103, University of Connecticut, Storrs, Conn. 06268 (U.S.A.).

FRANCE : M. J. HEURGON, Membre de l'Institut, Le Verger, Allée de la Pavillonne, F.-78170 La-Celle-St-Cloud.

ITALIE : Mlle M. L. PALADINI, 13, Via Bellotti, I.-20129 Milano.

IMPRIMERIE UNIVERSA, B-9200 WETTEREN (BELGIQUE)

COLLECTION LATOMUS
Fondée par Marcel RENARD
VOLUME 204

Susan D. MARTIN

The Roman Jurists and the Organization of Private Building in the Late Republic and Early Empire

LATOMUS
REVUE D'ÉTUDES LATINES
BRUXELLES
1989

ISBN 2-87031-144-3
D/1988/0415/118

ACKNOWLEDGEMENTS

I am grateful for the help I have received from several sources. The American Academy in Rome and the Istituto di Diritto Romano in the Faculty of Law at the University of Rome have both generously allowed me access to their collections. The graduate school at the University of Tennessee, Knoxville, provided funds to support four months in Rome in the fall of 1984. The college of Liberal Arts has furnished support for the completion of this project. I would like to thank each of these institutions. My colleagues in the Department of Classics at the University of Tennessee have offered many helpful suggestions. I would like especially to thank four other colleagues for their valuable help and support during the completion of this project : Paul Barrette, Dorothy Habel, Henry Kratz and Lynn Kraynak (visiting professor in the Department of Classics, 1985-86). A special debt of gratitude is owed to Professor B. W. Frier of the University of Michigan who directed the dissertation from which this book has developed and continues to be a source of inspiration for all interested in Roman legal studies. I would also like to thank *Collection Latomus* and in particular Mme Jacqueline Dumortier-Bibauw for her kind attention. Of course, all faults in the manuscript are my own.

LIST OF ABBREVIATIONS

ANRW	*Aufstieg und Niedergang der römischen Welt*, ed. H. TEMPORINI (Berlin-New York, since 1972), cited by volume.
V. Arangio-Ruiz, *Resp.*	Vincenzo ARANGIO-RUIZ, *Responsabilità contrattuale in diritto romano* (2nd ed. Naples 1933 ; repr. 1958).
Basilica	*Basilicorum Libri LX*, ed. G. E. HEIMBACH *et al.* (Leipzig 1833-1870), cited by volume and page ; new edition begun by H. J. SCHELTEMA *et al.* (The Hague, since 1953), with text (BT) and scholia (BS) separate, cited by page.
G. Beseler, *Beiträge*	Gerhard VON BESELER, *Beiträge zur Kritik der römischen Rechtsquellen*, I (1910), II (1911), III (1913), IV (1920, all at Tübingen), V (Leipzig 1931).
C. A. Cannata, *Colpa*	Carlo Augusto CANNATA, *Per lo studio della responsabilità per colpa nel diritto romano classico* (Milan 1967/68).
CIL	*Corpus Inscriptionum Latinarum* (Berlin), cited by volume and inscription number.
D.	*Digesta* (*Corpus Iuris Civilis*, vol. I edd. T. MOMMSEN and P. KRÜGER, often reprinted).
F. M. De Robertis, *I Rapporti*	*I rapporti di lavoro in diritto romano* (Milan 1946).
FIRA	*Fontes Iuris Romani Anteiustiniani* 2nd ed. vol. I (ed. S. RICCOBONO, 1941/1968), vol. II (edd. I. BAVIERA and I. FURLANI, 1940-1964), vol. III (ed. V. ARANGIO-RUIZ, new ed. with appendix, 1968, all at Florence).
B. W. Frier, *LTIR*	Bruce W. FRIER, *Landlords and Tenants in Imperial Rome* (Princeton 1980).
B. W. Frier, *RRJ*	Bruce W. FRIER, *The Rise of the Roman Jurists, Studies in Cicero's Pro Caecina* (Princeton 1985).
ILLRP	Attilio DEGRASSI, *Inscriptiones Latinae Liberae Rei Publicae*, 2 vols. (2nd ed., Florence 1965 and 1963, respectively).

ILS — Hermann DESSAU, *Inscriptiones Latinae Selectae*, 3 vols. (Berlin 1892-1916 ; often reprinted).

M. Kaser, *RPR*^{2} — Max KASER, *Das römische Privatrecht*, 2 vols. (2nd ed., Munich 1971-1975).

M. Kaser, *RZ* — Max KASER, *Das römische Zivilprozessrecht* (Munich 1966).

H. Kaufmann — Horst KAUFMANN, *Die altrömische Miete* (Cologne-Graz 1964).

R. Knütel, *SP* — Rolf KNÜTEL, *Stipulatio poenae. Studien zur römischen Vertragstrafe* (Cologne 1976).

T. Mayer-Maly, *LC* — Theo MAYER-MALY, *Locatio conductio* (Vienna 1956).

O. Lenel, *EP* — Otto LENEL, *Das Edictum perpetuum* (3rd ed., Leipzig 1927 ; repr. Aalen 1956).

O. Lenel, *Paling.* — Otto LENEL, *Palingenesia iuris civilis*, 2 vols. (Leipzig 1889 ; repr. Graz 1960).

J. L. D. Pearse — Jefferson Lawrence Daniel PEARSE, *The Organisation of Roman Building during the Late Republic and Early Empire* (diss. Cambridge, 1974).

A. Pernice, *Labeo* — Alfred PERNICE, *Labeo, Römisches Privatrecht im ersten Jahrhundert der Kaiserzeit*, I (1873), II 1/2 (2nd ed. 1895-1900), III i (2nd ed. 1892 Halle ; all vols. repr., Aalen 1963).

RE — *Paulys Realencyclopädie der classischen Altertumswissenschaft*, ed. G. WISSOWA *et al.* (Stuttgart) cited by article and column number.

F. Schulz, *History* — Fritz SCHULZ, *History of Roman Legal Science* (Oxford 1946).

J. A. C. Thomas — John Anthony Charles THOMAS, "Reflections on Building Contracts" *RIDA* 18 (1971) 673-689.

A. Watson, *Obligations* — Alan WATSON, *The Law of Obligations in the Later Roman Republic* (Oxford 1965).

T. Wiegand — Theodor WIEGAND, "Die puteolanische Bauinschrift" in *Jahrb. f. Klass. Philol.* Suppl. xx (1894) 660-778.

Periodicals are cited according to the list of abbreviations found in M. Kaser, *RPR*^{2} I xix-xxx ; those not found in this list are abbreviated as in *L'Année Philologique.*

INTRODUCTION

Festinat calidus mulis gerulisque redemptor,
torquet nunc lapidem, nunc ingens machina tignum,
Horace, *Ep.* 2.2.72-73

As Horace describes the busy street life in Rome, he remarks upon the activity of a building contractor at work, a daily sight in Republican and Imperial Rome. The streets were crowded with mules hauling carts so loaded with building materials that they threatened to tumble over and crush passersby ([1]). The rapid pace of new construction at certain times in the Republic and Empire aroused the criticism of the citizenry, and Seneca and Juvenal both lament the crowded conditions and the huge, poorly constructed apartment blocks which arose to house the populace ([2]). Of course, the construction of private and public buildings served a variety of functions at Rome in addition to providing shelter for the growing population. Public works enhanced the quality of urban life and secured good will for the current regime : Statius found the construction of the Via Domitiana so impressive that he devoted a long passage to the process of laying the roadbed, while Frontinus considered the history of the construction and maintenance of the aqueducts worthy of a monograph ([3]). Building also had important commercial and social functions, and Cicero and Horace both allude to the increase in prestige which could accompany conspicuous private construction ([4]).

Yet despite the Romans' zeal for building, attempting to describe how they coordinated a typical construction project raises difficult questions about the organization of building in Roman antiquity, and in particular about the supply of materials and the availability and procurement of a work force. Fortunately, a number of recent studies on subjects related to building have

(1) MART. 5.22.5-8 ; JUV. 3.254-261.
(2) SEN. *Ep.* 90.8 ; JUV. 3.190-211.
(3) STAT. *Silv.* 4.3.40-58.
(4) CIC. *Q.fr.* 2.5.1 ; HOR. *Sat.* 2.3.307.

contributed a great deal to our understanding of the construction process. For example, the scholarship on brick stamps is a great aid in understanding how these building materials were produced, by whom, and in what volume ([5]). Recently, several discussions of the epigraphic and literary evidence for the organization of building projects and workers have appeared ([6]). Studies of building techniques have raised such issues as how much skill was required for a typical Roman building, and to what extent an increase in demand might have changed the methods of construction ([7]). But much of the available evidence is too sparse or problematic to help in the elusive task of establishing connections between random pieces of evidence in order to understand the configuration of Roman construction.

In this study, I have undertaken the analysis of an abundant, yet unstudied, source for the organization and execution of construction. Justinian's *Digest* preserves a large number of excerpts from the writings of the classical Roman jurists (50 B.C.-A.D. 250) that deal with legal problems arising from building contracts. These texts provide valuable information both for the history of Roman construction and for the history of juristic law because they offer the possibility of viewing the development of a specific area of law within a social and economic context. The core of this study is legal analysis : it began as a doctoral dissertation in which I reconstructed from the juristic sources the structure of building contracts and the types of problems they posed to the jurists ([8]). In the present work, my first concern has also been to describe the substance of the juristic law : the rules and norms developed by the jurists to govern the activities of the contracting parties. However, I also attempt to explore how the law in this area developed as an integral and functioning part of its social and economic context, and in particular in regard to the dynamics of the Roman building trade. Consideration of the

(5) A convenient bibliography is in J. Bodel, *Roman Brick Stamps in the Kelsey Museum* (1983) 13-15. There is a lack of consensus in the scholarship on organizational aspects of brick production. For a summary, see especially M. Steinby, *Tituli* 4 (*Epigrafia e Ordine Senatorio*) (1982) 227-237 ; *ARID* Suppl. x-xi (1983) 219-221, with valuable observations about the organization of Roman construction.

(6) See especially J. L. D. Pearse, chapters 1-4. Most recently, P. A. Brunt, *JRS* 70 (1980) 81-100, discusses much of the evidence for the organization of public works.

(7) On the level of skill necessary in *opus caementicium*, F. Rakob, in *Hellenismus in Mittelitalien* (1976) 366-386. On changes in building methods, F. Coarelli, *PBSR* 45 (1977) 1-23 ; M. Torelli, in *Tecnologia, economica e società nel mondo romano* (1979) 139-159.

(8) S. D. Martin, *Building Contracts in Classical Roman Law* (diss. University of Michigan, 1981).

social and economic dimensions of the law will, I hope, shed new light on the position of contractors in the building trade and the importance of their participation in the 'legal culture' of Rome ([9]).

Most of the evidence for disputes between builders and employers comes from the jurists' discussion of the two commonly used forms of contract, *locatio conductio* and *stipulatio.* All these texts presume the existence of a contract with certain characteristics : an agreement between two individuals whereby one promises to build a specified immovable upon property furnished by the other. Because no thorough treatment of building contracts in Roman law has so far been attempted, it seemed best to proceed as methodically as possible in describing the contract itself and the problems which led the parties to seek the opinions of jurists ([10]). Therefore, I have begun by recreating the possible configurations of each type of contract at the moment of formation. No example of a private construction contract has survived from Roman Italy, and I have derived the model of a typical contract presented in Chapter I by inference from the juristic texts and from the supporting epigraphic and literary evidence attesting procedure in public contracting. The rest of the legal analysis is set out in Chapter III in a series of sections devoted to individual problems represented in the texts. The most significant legal issues involve the contractor's delay and his liability for the work both during the contract period and at the completion of the work. Two shorter sections discuss problems associated with the builder's payment, arrangements for securing the contract and provisions for fixed damages.

The main goal of the legal analysis has been to establish "the definitions and premises, methods and principles which will permit us to view the propositions of law which make up the preceptual element of the legal order (or any part of this) as a self-consistent system, or to increase our awareness of the logical relations between them" ([11]). The aim of this type of analytical jurisprudence is to represent a subsystem of the legal system in the fullest possible 'representation' : "assumptions hidden in the order of norms are

(9) L. FRIEDMAN, *Law and Society, An Introduction* (1977) 6-7, characterizes legal systems as consisting of substance, legal culture and structure. Substance is made up of rules and norms. Legal culture embodies the attitudes of the culture towards the legal system. The structure consists of the institutional organization of the legal system.

(10) Two previous studies have examined some of the relevant juristic sources in the context of building contracts : J. A. C. THOMAS, 673-689, and C. A. CANNATA, *Colpa* 135-240. Both authors are concerned only with limited aspects of the problems associated with these contracts.

(11) J. STONE, *Legal System and Lawyers' Reasonings* (1964) 41.

exposed ; the hierarchical structure of the order appears" ([12]). The benefit of this analysis is its ability to expose the range of juristic logic and reasoning, as well as the limitations of juristic thought ; it also serves to outline some, although perhaps not all, of the basic issues current in legal discussion and provides a point of departure for further analysis.

There are, however, drawbacks to this method which cannot be ignored. The picture it presents of the law is doubtless distorted through excessive rationality, and this distortion misrepresents both the process of juristic law-making and the daily workings of the law ([13]). In spite of these limitations, however, an important consideration necessitates a traditional, analytical approach to the sources. The selection of a topic like building contracts involves a significant shift of emphasis away from earlier trends in legal scholarship. Until quite recently, it has been common to analyze Digest sources either as they relate to large, procedural categories, or within discussions of broad concepts such as risk or negligence ([14]). A number of the texts discussed in this work have been extensively analyzed in these contexts. Scholars have been influenced to a great extent by the form imposed upon the texts by Justinian's compilers. Divorced from their original contexts and abbreviated, so as to eliminate signs of controversy among the ancient jurists, the texts were arranged under titles corresponding to available actions. For example, all cases which are tried under the *actio locati* are collected in title 19.2. Scholars have tended to presuppose that the Roman jurists themselves formulated legal opinions guided by the rigorous use of these categories. This underlying conviction has provided the justification for seeking a unified concept of *locatio conductio* which can be applied to the study of all types of activities made actionable by this contract. The search for rational, coherent categories has generated studies of *locatio conductio* (although they are not numerous), but not of topics selected according to individual contractual activities ([15]). In addition, many of the texts pertaining to construction have not fully escaped the burdensome censure of "Interpola-

(12) R. MOORE, *Legal Norms and Legal Science* (1978) 35.

(13) R. MOORE (cited note 12), 35. B. W. FRIER, *LTIR* 200-202 ; 174-175, discusses this problem in relationship to reconstructing landlord and tenant law from *Digest* sources.

(14) The most frequently discussed topic is *periculum*, or risk for loss, see below, Chapter III, section B.

(15) See above all, T. MAYER-MALY, *LC*, and H. KAUFMANN. On the paucity of treatments of *locatio conductio*, see M. KASER, *SZ* 73 (1956) 424-431. *Locatio conductio operis* is underrepresented in the scholarship. Studies of legal topics selected with reference to important segments of Roman economy and society are gaining acceptance, see, for example, B. W. FRIER, *LTIR*, and G. RICKMAN, *Roman Granaries and Store Buildings* (1971).

tionskritik", the search for Justinianic or pre-Justinianic alterations of the sources ([16]). The result of all this is that these texts have never been examined as a coherent system. This factor alone justifies a complete reappraisal of these sources.

A further problem is that much scholarly discussion of jurists' law assumes that their law-making was a relatively static, scientific process of conceptual development, a view encouraged, as I mentioned above, by the form in which the sources have come down to us. As A. A. Schiller pointed out a number of years ago, scholars of Roman law still seek to inhabit Jhering's 'heaven of legal concepts' ([17]). But this approach obscures the real quality and achievement of juristic law-making. Max Kaser has demonstrated that the Roman jurists worked on a case-by-case basis following a pattern of reasoning similar to that found in Common Law systems ([18]). The jurists developed categories and concepts through a process of reasoning by analogy from case to case in a way which was imperfectly inductive but certainly not deductive ([19]). As the inventors of autonomous legal reasoning, they were concerned with the creation of a legal language adequate to express and perpetuate a system of norms which they created. But, as B. W. Frier has recently stressed, they were in no sense 'scientific policymakers' or exponents of legal science in the sense in which European jurists have been in modern times ([20]). Therefore, the law developed slowly in specific areas as new and difficult cases reached the jurists either through legal debate or from the courts. Lines of thought underwent change and modification over time both as a result of legal discourse and as factors external to the legal system increasingly placed demands upon the courts.

(16) I have adopted a conservative approach to the search for interpolations in the texts under examination here. By this I mean that I have been reluctant to discount the evidence of *Digest* texts on the grounds of presumed interpolations and have proceeded from the assumption that many texts are classical in content although perhaps altered in form as M. KASER has argued, *Zur Methodologie der römischen Rechtsquellenforschung* in *SAWW* 277 (1972) and *La critica del testo. Atti del secondo Congresso internazionale della Società italiana di storia del diritto* (1971) I 291 ; 340-341. However, it is also important to take into account the important criticisms of F. WIEACKER, *Textstufen klassischer Juristen* (1960) 172-174. For further discussion, see F. WIEACKER, *SZ* 91 (1974) 1-40, and A. A. SCHILLER, *Roman Law, Mechanisms of Development* (1978) 62-72.

(17) A. A. SCHILLER, *Columbia Law Review* 58 (1958) 1237.

(18) M. KASER, *Zur Methode der römischen Rechtsfindung* in *NAWG* (1962) 49-78.

(19) E. LEVI, *An Introduction to Legal Reasoning* (1949) 1-6 ; 19.

(20) B. W. FRIER, *LTIR* 46-47, relying upon the distinction between 'Scientific Policymaker' and 'Ordinary Observer' drawn by B. ACKERMANN, *Private Property and the Constitution* (1977) 185-189.

I have attempted to mitigate the remote quality of the legal analysis by focusing upon the background to the legal disputes and the effect of the development of jurisprudence upon the expectations and legal positions of the parties. Despite the rather dry character of the juristic texts, cases arising from building contracts were fraught with difficult situations in which the expectations of the parties were thwarted or delayed. Indeed, it seems that building contracts tend to generate lawsuits because of several inherent characteristics. The contract creates a relationship between people who have no other contact : they meet and come to terms for a project of limited duration. The parties may often be of different social status and unlikely to have access to extra-legal methods of dispute settlement ([21]). In addition, building can be risky. It requires a substantial capital outlay on the part of the employer, and an investment in time (and lost opportunities) by the contractor. The process of building tends to be slow, labor intensive, seasonal, expensive and vulnerable to vicissitudes of nature ([22]). Things often go wrong, and the parties may attempt to mitigate the possibilities of loss in different ways. The employer attempts to ensure his legal protection from the outset by the use of additional contract clauses and of sureties. Builders may be reluctant to put all of their time into one project, and may attempt to work on more than one job at a time. It is vital to our understanding to keep in mind that the reality which furnished the impetus to law at Rome, although largely lost to us, was potentially quite tumultuous.

In accordance with these considerations, I have tried in Chapter II to reconstruct the social and economic environment which gave rise to the law on construction. The building scene at Rome was characterized by a variety of ways of organizing skilled and unskilled workers to accomplish individual projects, and among these, the use of slave labor and the hire of day laborers or of contractors were doubtless popular alternatives. In spite of the lack of unambiguous and explicit testimony for the activities of builders, evidence

(21) See D. Black, *The Behavior of Law* (1976) 15, on the increased likelihood of litigation between members of different ranks ; on Black, D. F. Greenberg, *Law and Society Review* 17 (1983) 337-390. L. Friedman, *Contract Law in America* (1965) 43 and 48-49, remarks that in Wisconsin of the mid-nineteenth century and early twentieth century, building contracts generated a great deal of litigation but that these suits were usually brought by or against smaller contractors engaging in one-time arrangements with their employers. The tendency towards increased rationalization of the construction industry diminished the chance that parties would end up in court.

(22) On the characteristics of construction and the implications of this for modern organization of the industry, see P. J. Cassimatis, *The Economics of the Construction Industry* in *Studies in Business Economics* 111 (1969) 12-17.

such as the growth and prominence of the *collegium* of the *fabri tignarii* at Rome and at Ostia indicates that there were many builders at work, some achieving a moderate degree of prosperity. The most successful were probably those who worked on public projects. But the evidence for private building on a large scale, such as we can see at Ostia, demonstrates that a sizable number of builders were employed by private individuals. Unfortunately, there is no way to determine how the majority of construction jobs were organized. But the presence of an active construction trade seems secure ([23]).

Finally, Chapter IV is concerned with an analysis of how the legal system dealt with two competing and fairly well-defined interest groups ([24]). In arriving at their opinions, the jurists balanced claims arising between people with rather different positions in society and opposing views of what the contract was to do. The employers tend to be landowners, a potentially powerful group, whose concern is to obtain from the builder a structure in as nearly perfect condition as possible. Builders provide the expert knowledge necessary to fulfill a basic need : they gain their livelihood in this way. My general observation has been that the jurists were moving away from an early tendency to hold the builder strictly liable for his work towards a law of contract with more complexly differentiated rights and duties. In the early stages of juristic consideration of these contracts, the employer's interpretation of the contract and of the completed structure probably furnished the standard used to measure the builder's work. But the sources demonstrate that jurists' law begins to give to builders more access to the legal system and more ways to defend claims. This is done through a variety of techniques. For example, many disputes arose from disagreements about the quality of the finished product, and the jurists frequently mediated between the landowner's standard of perfection and the builder's level of performance. The jurists began to use standards in the trade as guidelines for establishing levels of competency. This implies an awareness of the existence of a building trade capable of providing such information, and it is conceivable that the law on building contracts increasingly was formulated to regulate and standardize the level of performance expected from builders.

(23) I use the phrase 'construction trade' in the widest possible sense to indicate the totality of individuals who provided skilled construction work regardless of title or mode of employ. By the use of the term 'trade', I do not mean to indicate that construction workers functioned in an organized manner to promote homogeneous concerns.

(24) I have relied upon the model of the legal system in L. FRIEDMAN (cited at note 9) and *The Legal System* (1975), especially Chapters 1 and 4, (see further below at Chapter IV).

This pattern of interests assumes an active role for building contractors in defining and pressing claims, and this may seem surprising. It has long been thought that Roman legal culture favored upper class claims and was generally not accessible to members of the lower status groups in society ([25]). Much of the substance of Roman law is of concern primarily to the upper ranks of society, and they stood to benefit most from the use of the legal system ([26]). But the concerns of Roman law do not perfectly mirror those of the upper class as defined by status, and extend to a wider group, those belonging to a commercial class with an interest in using the legal system ([27]). It seems possible that building contractors, who were not members of the upper levels of society, nevertheless were sufficiently active in the economic sphere to gain access to the legal system.

Legal culture also places barriers in the way of potential litigants in the structure and substance of the legal system. Claimants will decide whether or not to proceed with an action based upon their perceptions of the ease and utility of the system : how difficult is it to bring the claim to court ? What are their chances of winning ? Can they risk losing ? Will the financial costs of litigation outweight the potential advantages ([28]) ? The evidence from the *Digest* indicates that claims by parties to construction constracts were successful in penetrating these screening factors. We can therefore suppose that some builders possessed the minimum level of legal sophistication necessary to manipulate the legal system, and that they were sufficiently differentiated and remote from their employers to be able to exercise claims in this way.

Much of the legal activity in this area may be attributed to the conditions prevalent in the early Empire, which was remarkable for the amount of building activity taking place both publicly and privately, organized by contracts and in other ways. This surge in building, especially under Trajan

(25) For example, P. GARNSEY, *Social Status and Legal Privilege in the Roman Empire* (1970). L. FRIEDMAN (cited note 9), 7, defines legal culture as the prevalent "ideas, attitudes, beliefs, expectations, and opinions about law", and further notes that legal culture can screen out or divert many disputes from the courts depending upon the parties' expectations.

(26) D. DAUBE, *Roman Law, Linguistic, Social and Philosophical Aspects* (1969) 65-128, has demonstrated that the utility of certain areas of Roman law was restricted to the upper classes. The failure of Roman law to develop in areas like labor law is also cited as an example of its upper class bias. The pervasiveness of this characteristic of Roman law is, however, widely debated and deserves further careful consideration.

(27) This prosperous class is not identical with the status elite, see K. P. JOHNE, *Gnomon* 55 (1983) 138-141, and B. W. FRIER, *LTIR*, chapters 1 and 2.

(28) On the screening factors imposed by structure and substance, see L. FRIEDMAN (cited note 9), 6-7.

and Hadrian, led to an increasing number of people being employed to supply the building needs of the state and of private individuals ([29]). Our knowledge of these craftsmen is very limited, and it is only in the law that we can see traces of the activities of the builders themselves for whom the contracting business was a good source of livelihood, but also a risky one which generated litigation.

(29) On the general increase in productivity and in the numbers of craftspeople, see K. Hopkins in *Trade in the Ancient Economy* (edd. P. Garnsey, K. Hopkins, C. R. Whittaker, 1983), Introduction xiv-xxi.

CHAPTER I

The Formation of a Building Contract

I. – Introduction

The landowner desiring to improve his property by adding a building must coordinate the supply and organization of three basic components : technical skill, labor and materials for the construction. One common solution to the organizational problems of building has been to contract with a professional builder who agrees to undertake the job either in part or as a whole. Contracting can embrace a variety of ways of balancing and distributing the responsibilities for the various parts of the job, and an employer can chose his degree of participation depending upon how much control he wishes to assume on a day-to-day basis. For example, a builder can be hired to work in his own area of specialization with a few other builders, so that he undertakes no particular responsibility for the whole project. Other alternatives involve an increasing level of control by the builder in the totality of the building process. Often, contracting allows the employer to transfer to a skilled professional all or most of the responsibility for organizing the job, thereby avoiding extensive personal involvement in the process of construction ([1]).

The formation of the contract is the moment when detailed decisions about the organization of the project are embodied in an agreement. The Romans used one of two available contracts, *locatio conductio* or *stipulatio.* In both types of contract, the fundamental components of the obligation are the same : the employer furnishes to the contractor a plan for the building and a piece of land, usually his own. It is not essential that the employer be the owner of the land ; he could be acting on behalf of the actual owner

(1) On the constituent parts of any building project, R. Goldthwaite, *The Building of Renaissance Florence* (1980) 115, has a historical overview of various methods of organizing construction emphasizing the difference between contractual modes and 'totalitarian' modes involving slave or forced labor. I have also relied on E. W. Cooney, *Economic History Review* 8 (1955-56) 167-168, who lists four types of relationships between the builder and the owner of the building site.

through mandate or some other arrangement. The builder brings his expertise to the project and acquires no property rights either in the land or the building through the contract (2).

The early use of construction contracts by private individuals is difficult to document. *Stipulatio* as a method of forming contracts was in use early in Roman law (3). But jurists' law produces no explicit examples of construction contracts concluded through stipulation before the first century A.D. In D.45.1.72 pr., Ulpian cites the early imperial jurist Tubero on the general problem of the division of stipulations for obligations 'to do' (*facere*) when the content seems incapable of being divided (4). Ulpian includes construction as one example of such a stipulation, and although it is impossible to determine from this that construction was among the obligations *facere* in the Republic, it seems likely that it was.

This text typifies the characteristics of jurists' law in reference to *stipulatio*. *Stipulatio* was a method whereby any promise could be made actionable by the verbal exchange of a question and answer. The number of possible contractual activities is manifold, and jurisprudence in this area tends to read like a law of contract, establishing rules for valid formation and categorizing types of obligations. Stipulations for construction often furnish examples in discussions of the category of obligations *facere*, which develop characteristic areas of controversy such as delay and calculation of the value of the obligation. Only rarely did one specific contractual activity develop implied terms peculiar to itself (5).

Locatio conductio differs from *stipulatio* in the requirements for formation and in the character and typical content of the obligation. A valid contract in *locatio conductio* required the agreement of the parties upon the terms of the contractual activities and a fixed price (see further below). The use of *locatio* was restricted to a sphere of activities encompassed in the two verbs *locare* and *conducere*: the *locator* 'placed' his job, thing or day of work with the *conductor* who undertook to work at the job, use the thing or labor for

(2) Other patterns of land development by employers are investigated in Chapter II. The jurists are explicit on the builder's lack of property interest in either the building materials or building site, see below on D.19.2.22.1-2 and D.18.1.20.

(3) A. WATSON, *Obligations* 1-6 ; B. BIONDI, *Contratto e stipulatio* (1953) 273-291.

(4) ULPIAN, (20 *ad ed.*) D.45.1.72 pr., see A. WATSON, *Obligations* 6. On this jurist, E. KLEBS, *RE* s.v. Aelius # 156 col. 537-538 (1894).

(5) On the failure of *stipulatio* to develop many implied terms, see A. WATSON, *Obligations* 1-6. While the texts on construction tend to be discussed in reference to generic problems, such as the attributes of an obligation *facere* or discussions of invalid formation, they also develop an implied term in the area of delay.

a day, according to the terms of the contract. Thus, unlike *stipulatio*, which furnished a formal method of validitating a variety of contractual activities, *locatio conductio* developed in regard to specific activities such as the lease of habitations or granaries, hire of a day laborer and hire of an artisan.

Building contracts in *locatio conductio* were in use by the time of Cato, and both he and Cicero furnish important examples of the use of *locatio conductio* for construction (6). Although the early history of *locatio* is murky, a number of significant economic activities fell under the purview of the contract, such as lease of dwellings or other immovables. By the late Republic, cases arising from *locationes* begin to interest the jurists. In regard to construction, the earliest relevant text comes from the Republican jurist Alfenus Varus (D.19.2.30.3), and the main characteristics of the contract discernable in later sources are already established by this time. The jurists of the early empire, and in particular Labeo and Sabinus, play an important role in framing the discussion of the parties' liabilities (7). By the end of the first century A.D., a well-defined set of problems in construction law had emerged in the writings of the jurists. Because the juristic discussion focuses upon construction as a well-differentiated type within *locatio conductio*, a more detailed and complex account of this contract is possible, and this relative wealth of detail contrasts sharply with the texts on *stipulatio* which tend to stress general rules for the validation and enforcement of promises.

The Romans had also been accustomed to contracting, specifically through *locatio-conductio*, as a way of accomplishing a variety of public works, from road construction to supplying the army. Numerous texts, both literary and epigraphic, document the general procedure : a magistrate (censor, consul, aedile or urban praetor) let contracts to one or more *redemptores* in an auction ; outside of Rome, *duouiri* and *duouirales* administered contracts (8).

(6) CATO, *Agr.* 14 ; see U. VON LÜBTOW, *Symbolae Raphaeli Taubenschlag dedicatae* III (1957) = *Eos* 48, 3 (1956) 227-241, especially at 232-233 ; A. WATSON, *Obligations* 139-140 ; H. KAUFMANN, 205-216. P. THIELSCHER, *Des Marcus Cato Belehrung über die Landwirtschaft* (1963) 222-223, doubts that a building contract is being used. On Cicero's use of contractors, see Chapter II.

(7) LABEO : (4 *post. a Jau. epit.*) D.19.2.58.1 ; (5 *post. a Jau. epit.*) D.19.2.60.3 and 4 ; (1 *pith.*) D.19.2.62. Sabinus is cited in Javolenus' epitome of Labeo's *Posteriores*, D.19.2.59.

(8) Consul : *CIL* 1^2 694 ; Aedile : *CIL* 1^2 1560 ; *ILLRP* 449 ; Censors : LIVY 45.15.9 ; Praetor : CIC. 2 *Verr.* i. 130. *Duouiri* and *duouirales* : *FIRA* III # 153 = *ILLRP* 518. The most valuable sources on public contracting are the *lex parieti faciundo Puteolana*, *FIRA* III # 153 = *ILLRP* 518 ; CIC. 2 *Verr.* i 130-150 ; two municipal charters, *FIRA* I # 21 = *ILS* 6087 and *FIRA* I # 24 = *ILS* 6089. For other epigraphic references, see A. BISCARDI, *DE* s.v. *locatio.* See also E. BADIAN, *Publicans and Sinners* (1972), and J. L. D. PEARSE, ch. 1.

These magistrates, or specially appointed surrogates, were to oversee the completion and approval of the work. The extent to which contracting remained in use in public works in the Empire is disputed, although there is evidence to suggest that contractors continued to play a role into the second century A.D. ([9]).

For all periods, the non-legal sources for public building are much more numerous than those for private projects and they are, therefore, valuable for the purposes of this study. But since the administration of public law was in the hands of magistrates who exercised their own discretion in managing the execution of contracts, these sources do not provide any information about private law adjudication of claims or the development of jurisprudence in this area. Although public contracting cannot furnish evidence about the legal treatment of private contractors, the formal similarities between the two systems are striking, and public contracting provides a valuable structural model for the configuration of the contracts. So while frequent use will be made of these sources, their value is restricted to furnishing possible analogies to private practice ([10]).

II. – *STIPVLATIO*

Stipulatio was a formal, verbal contract, requiring the oral exchange of a question and answer. The stipulator (the promissee) framed the obligation in the form of a question. Papinian gives an example of a sample *stipulatio* for the construction of a building : *insulam intra biennium illo loco aedificari spondes ?* ([11]). The promissor usually responded : *spondeo.* Other word usage was accepted provided that both parties used the same verb, but it is likely that the traditional words were most commonly used ([12]). Because the

(9) P. A. BRUNT, *JRS* 70 (1980) 84-88. See further below at Chapter II, Section III.

(10) I am leaving aside the problems associated with the origins of *locatio conductio,* especially those involving assigning priority in time to the public or private form. My account is only concerned with the juristic law beginning in the first century B.C. For a review of the scholarship on the early history of *locatio conductio,* see M. KASER, *RPR*[2] I 562-565, and H. KAUFMANN, 265-275. The public contracting system was regulated by magisterial law and therefore was conducted along very different lines. On L. Amirante's theory of the late development of *locatio conductio operis,* see below at note 63.

(11) PAPINIAN, (2 *definitionum*) D.45.1.124. For a general discussion of *stipulatio,* see M. KASER, *RPR*[2] I 538-543 ; S. RICCOBONO-J. KERR-WYLIE-B. BEINART, *Stipulation and the Theory of Contracts* (1957) chapter 2 ; B. BIONDI (cited note 3), 269-385 ; G. GROSSO, *Il sistema romano dei contratti*[3] (1963) 127-132 ; P. VOCI, *La dottrina romana del contratto* (1946) 131-136 ; A. WATSON, *Obligations* 1-9.

(12) The response often consisted of one word (CIC. *Caec.* 3.7). The verb used in the oral question was usually repeated in the answer, see Gaius 3.92 : *uerbis obligatio fit ex interro-*

contract was formal, its validity depended upon the precise execution of the verbal promise. For example, a failure to respond or to name expressly the same thing or sum, generally resulted in invalidity ([13]). The parties also had to be legally capable of entering into a contract. In addition to the usual rules about legal capacity, for example, all parties had to be sane and of age (or procure a tutor's authorization), there was the further requirement that neither party be deaf, mute or an infant. In such cases, the contract could still be formed by giving an order to a slave who spoke the necessary words ([14]).

In *stipulatio* one party bound himself to fulfill a promise put to him by the stipulator. The legal sources are unclear as to how this unilateral contract provided for a corresponding obligation. For example, the builder promises to construct an *insula* ; how does he secure the reciprocal obligation for payment from the employer ? Two possible solutions suggest themselves : the parties could conclude another stipulation binding the previous stipulator to pay a certain amount to the builder. Alternatively, the stipulation could include provisions for pay and other reciprocal obligations among its terms ([15]). Unfortunately, the legal texts only offer simplified examples too brief to indicate how this inherent difficulty was surmounted in practice. At least one written example of a stipulation survives in which complex reciprocal provisions are agreed upon and made actionable when the stipulator states the promise and the promissor responds. Such written documents were commonplace. They were not considered 'the contract' but served only as evidence of the parties' agreement ([16]).

gatione et responsione, ueluti : 'dari spondes ? spondeo, dabis ? dabo'. See also *PS* 2.3. But this may not have been essential, see Ulpian, D.45.1.1.2, and B. Biondi (cited note 3), 300.

(13) Gaius 3.102, states this explicitly ; see also Paul, D.45.1.83.2. Opinions are divided as to what happens if the parties stipulate for two different sums, Ulpian, D.45.1.1.4, and Paul, D.45.1.83.3. See B. Biondi (cited note 3), 299-300.

(14) Ulpian, D.45.1.1 pr. ; Gaius 3.104-109. See B. Biondi (cited note 3), 296.

(15) C. A. Cannata, *Colpa* 164, assumed that the parties resolved this by concluding another stipulation binding the stipulator to pay a certain amount. There is support in the scholarship for the idea that either one or a pair of stipulations could be formulated to contain reciprocal terms, see H. Kaufmann, 340-341, who relies upon V. Arangio-Ruiz, *La compravendita in diritto romano* I 2nd. ed. (1954 ; repr. 1961) 62-71, and D. Daube, *SZ* 66 (1948) 91-134. Daube demonstrated that through novation stipulations can acquire all the characteristics of the previous agreement including *bona fides.* See also L. Amirante, *Iura* 16 (1965) 330 n. 2.

(16) *FIRA* III # 157 records the recasting of a partnership for lending money (*societas*) into a stipulation. On the value of the written record of the agreement, see B. Nicholas, *LQR* 69 (1953) 233-240. Such records must have been commonplace, see Cicero, *Att.* 12.17 ; *Top.* 26.96 ; cf. *Auctor ad Her.* 2.9.13 ; 2.10.14.

At the conclusion of the oral promise, the obligation was actionable through the *actio ex stipulatu.* This was the appropriate action when the stipulation was for an *incertum,* something not quantifiable in terms of a fixed sum (*certa pecunia*) or a specific object (*certa res*). Ulpian placed stipulations for construction specifically in this category ([17]). The formula is partially preserved by Gaius (4.136):

> *Iudex esto. Quod A. Agerius de N. Negidio incertum stipulatus est, cuius rei dies fuit, quidquid ob eam rem N. Negidium A. Agerio dare facere oportet (eius iudex N. Negidium A. Agerio condemnato ; si non paret, absoluito)* ([18]).

The *actio ex stipulatu* was younger than the *condictio,* the action used to sue for a *certum,* but the formula was probably known by the time of Plautus ([19]). This action was *stricti iuris* which meant that the *iudex* was to evaluate strictly the performance of the defendant according to the letter of the agreement. The major exception to this strict interpretation was afforded by the *exceptio doli* which allowed the defendant to plead the plaintiff's fraud as a defense. Before the introduction of this *exceptio,* stipulation would have been a risky undertaking ([20]).

The formula calls for the *iudex* to determine *quidquid ... dare facere oportet,* and this phrase has suggested to many scholars that the *stipulatio incerti* may have been interpreted less literally than a *stipulatio* for a fixed sum or a specific object. This assumption depends especially upon the belief that good faith is implicit in *oportet* ([21]). The *iudex* must always interpret the

(17) ULPIAN, (22 *ad ed.*) D.45.1.75.7.

(18) O. LENEL, *EP* 151-154, restores the portion after *oportet*; he believed that the *demonstratio* would have always been as Gaius records it, omitting mention of the basis of the stipulation. M. KASER, *RZ* 241 notes 27 and 28 and *RPR*[2] I 542 n. 42, disagrees and feels that the content of the obligation was included ; further on the formula, see KASER, *Labeo* 22 (1976) 7-29.

(19) For the relative youth of the *stipulatio incerti,* see M. KASER, *RZ* 79 n. 18, with examples from Plautus and Cato and H. KAUFMANN, 337-342, with bibliography.

(20) The *exceptio doli* may date to the mid 70's B.C., B. W. FRIER, *RRJ* 148 n. 39 on CICERO, *N.D.* 3.74 ; cp. A. WATSON, *Law Making in the Later Roman Republic* (1974) 72-75. There were also the *exceptiones metus* and *pacti,* see M. KASER, *RPR*[2] I 487-489.

(21) The wider room for interpretation allowed by the *actio ex stipulatu* has often been noticed : M. KASER, *RPR*[2] I 506 n. 22. An important example of this is found in VENULEIUS, (1 *stip.*) D.45.1.137.2-3, see below Chapter III, section A. On this, C. A. CANNATA, *Colpa* 152-163 ; V. ARANGIO RUIZ (cited note 15), 181 ; M. KASER, *RZ* 111 n. 35 with bibliography. F. PASTORI, *Appunti in tema di sponsio e stipulatio* (1961) 185-215, has hypothesized, on the basis of the *lex de Gallia Cisalpina* (*FIRA* I # 19), that the *actio ex stipulatu* originally contained the words *ex bona fide.* When, at a later date, *stipulatio* and *sponsio* were merged in the *ius ciuile,* the formula became *stricti iuris.* This view has not been accepted, cf. A. MAGDELAIN, *Iura* 13 (1962) 287-290, and M. TALAMANCA, *Labeo* 9 (1963) 96-117.

words of the contract, but can also consider whether the defendant has done what he "ought" to have done. This would allow the *iudex* to use discretion in evaluating the performance of the defendant. In general, stipulations for construction are subjected to literal interpretation when the suit is brought with reference to a specific clause in the contract. In the absence of a specific clause, the jurists may resort to filling the missing component based upon what a 'good man' would consider reasonable ([22]).

In addition to the general requirements for validity discussed above, stipulations for construction also had to include some reference to the specific location of the construction site :

Ulpian, (27 *ad ed.*) D.13.4.2.5

Si quis insulam fieri stipuletur et locum non adiciat, non ualet stipulatio.

The text has not been considered interpolated ([23]). Ulpian specifically places the burden upon the stipulator to make clear the location of the site. This could be named explicitly in the promise as in D.45.1.124 (see above p. 22). In D.45.1.115 pr., Papinian counts as *imperfecta* a stipulation made *non demonstrato loco.* This wording suggests that the employer could show the builder the site, and perhaps it was customary both to view the land and to make a note of the location in the promise ([24]). In any case, failure to indicate the building site results in invalidity. The reason for this rule seems commonsensical : how can the promissor undertake a construction project when the site itself is unknown ? The stipulator, as the one who formulates the content of the obligation, is required to supply enough information to allow the promissor to fulfill his promise. If the contract did contain a specific reference to the location of the building site, the builder who built in the wrong location would be held liable in an action ([25]).

(22) See below at Chapter III, section A.

(23) See the *Index Interpolationum.*

(24) PAPINIAN, (2 *quaest.*) D.45.1.115 pr. : *uel insulam aedificari non demonstrato loco. Demonstrare* is used in the expression *demonstrare fines,* to indicate an inspection of the boundaries of parcels of land, usually prior to a sale : POMPONIUS, (9 *ad Sab.*) D.18.1.18.1 ; ALFENUS, (4 *dig. a Paulo epit.*) D.21.1.45. Perhaps the pointing out of the building site was a customary precursor to a stipulation for construction. C. A. CANNATA, *Colpa* 149-150, thinks Papinian's rule too rigid in light of D.45.1.95 discussed below. See also M. KASER, *RPR*[2] I 249 n. 30.

(25) If the builder builds on the wrong site, he has not discharged his obligation, see ULPIAN, (27 *ad ed.*) D.13.4.2.7, citing Marcellus. C. A. CANNATA, *Colpa* 150.

Another text approaches the problem from a different point of view :

Marcellus, (5 *digestorum*) D.45.1.95

Qui insulam fieri stipulatur, ita demum adquirit obligationem, si apparet, quo in loco fieri insulam uoluerit : si et ibi insulam fieri interest eius.

Marcellus states that a stipulation to construct an *insula* can be valid if it is apparent where the building is to be placed, and if the stipulator has an interest in the building of an *insula* on that site. The last sentence of the text is usually considered interpolated since most scholars have preferred not to accept as classical the notion that an agreement lacking a necessary clause can be validated by relying upon the stipulator's 'interest' in a certain project. But there is no compelling reason to doubt the form or language of the text ([26]).

The case presupposes the formation of a stipulation for the construction of an *insula,* but implies that the building site has been omitted from the oral promise. There has not been a mistake concerning the place, it simply has not been mentioned. Marcellus is willing to grant validity to such an agreement provided that two conditions are met. First, the location of the building site must have been evident at the time of the formation of the agreement. If a written record of the stipulation included this information, this evidence would be persuasive. However, the problem underlying this case may have been precisely that no written documentary evidence of the promise was available. Marcellus may have considered it sufficient that the location had been pointed out to the builder ([27]).

Second, the jurist states that if the stipulator had an interest in the construction of an *insula* on that spot, this fact validated the agreement. It is difficult to tell whether this condition depends upon the fulfillment of the first one or independently can suffice to validate the agreement. Perhaps Marcellus intended the information concerning the stipulator's 'interest' in the construction to support other types of evidence of the validity of the agreement, such as pointing out the site. The builder might attempt to establish, for example, that the employer owned the site and therefore had

(26) G. BESELER, *TR* 10 (1930) 188, and A. PERNICE, *Labeo* III.i 190, both bracket the last *si*-clause ; C. A. CANNATA, *Colpa* 149, accepts this alteration. Beseler would also substitute *adiciat* for *apparet* and then remove the end of the text after *uoluerit.*

(27) Marcellus may not therefore be contradicting Papinian if we read *demonstrare* as meaning 'to point out or show' (see note 24). The difficulty is presumably that no explicit mention of the site appears in any of the evidence pertaining to the contract.

an interest in its improvement. This text upholds the validity of a stipulation which lacks an explicit reference to the location of the construction site by establishing a minimum criterion for determining if there was sufficient information available about the site for the promissor to carry out the construction.

Another common feature of the stipulation was the provision for a completion date expressed either as a fixed day or as an interval of time at the end of which the obligation fell due ([28]). The absence of this provision did not invalidate the stipulation. The stipulator could bring an *actio ex stipulatu* if he thought the builder was requiring an excessively long time to complete the work. It was left to the *iudex* to determine whether or not the builder had defaulted on his obligation.

In addition to these two elements of the stipulation, there must have been specifications for the builder to follow in doing his work. The legal sources never mention any plans or written descriptions of the work, and references to the type of building usually consist of a single word. The *Digest* texts often read like hypothetical cases, especially in the area of *stipulatio,* because the jurists discuss generic problems rather than problems particular to individual contractual activities. A stipulation for an *insula* seems to have been the standard example of a construction contract and appears frequently in discussions of *stipulationes incerti* ([29]). C. A. Cannata inferred from these taciturn descriptions that *stipulatio* as a form was less suited than *locatio* to construction because it lacked *leges locationis* in which the specifications could be included ([30]). He is correct that *stipulatio* developed no *leges* modifying or extending the legal responsibilities of the parties, but this does not preclude the existence of instructions for the work. Since factual details rarely enter into the juristic discussion unless they are crucial parts of a dispute, there are relatively few references to individual projects even in *locatio.* We have already seen that epigraphical evidence demonstrates the

(28) For example, see D.45.1.124 : *intra biennium* ; D.45.1.72.1 : *ante kalendas Martias* ; D.45.1.113 pr. : *ante kalendas Iunias.* See below at Chapter III, section A, for further discussion of this issue.

(29) Typical examples are : D.5.1.43 (*insulam fieri*) ; D.13.4.2.5 (*insulam fieri*) ; D.45.1.14 (*insulam aedificare*) ; D.45.1.15 (*insula facta sit*) ; D.45.1.38.21 (*insulam faciendam promiserit*) ; D.45.1.72 pr. (*insulam fabricari*) ; D.45.1.72.2 (*insula fabricari possit*) ; D.45.1.84 (*insulam fieri*) ; D.45.1.95 (*insulam fieri*) ; D.45.1.115 pr. (*insulam aedificari*) ; D.45.1.124 (*insulam aedificari*) ; D.45.1.137.3 (*insulam fieri*) ; D.46.3.31 (*insulam aedificandam*). But see also D.45.1.14 (*domum aedificari*) ; D.45.1.73 pr. (*domum aedificari*) ; D.45.1.75.7 (*domum aedificari*).

(30) C. A. CANNATA, *Colpa* 137-140.

potential complexity of the underlying *causa* of the stipulation. There is ample evidence in non-legal sources that builders normally worked with plans and models designed by architects, and the remains of *insulae* at Ostia indicate the wide variety of different designs and of techniques used in construction ([31]). So we cannot exclude the possibility that specifications accompanied stipulations for construction.

A stipulation for the construction of a building consisted of these few elements cast in the form of a promise and imposed upon the parties few implied conditions, terms or obligations. For the most part, suits arising from stipulations were judged rather strictly according to the words of the agreement. The standard principle of interpretation was to follow "what was done" ([32]). If the words of the stipulation were ambiguous, the judge was to interpret this against the stipulator ([33]). In construction, many suits probably turned upon determining whether or not the builder had executed the plan for the building on time. Specific requirements formulated in the verbal promise tend to be enforced strictly with only a little room for interpretation. If there is a gap, such as the omission of the completion date, the jurists depart from this technique and are willing to consider circumstances surrounding the formation or execution of the contract in order to preserve the agreement (see further at Chapter III, section A).

III. – Ancillary Pacts

Stipulations have another important use in construction which derives from their flexibility and adaptability to a number of legal tasks. Often the parties to a contract would append stipulations to a principal contract. In construction, the standard practice was to use ancillary stipulations in two ways. The employer often chose to supplement construction contracts in

(31) The plans of *insulae* display individual characteristics based upon considerations of the building size and of the comfort of the future inhabitants. The construction techniques also show a wide range of quality. Compare, for example, at Ostia the plan of the Trajanic Cassette Tipo *insulae* (III. xii.1-2), which are quite shoddily built but have private latrines, and the later, standardized plan and construction in the Case a Giardino (III.ix), see J. Packer, *The Insulae of Imperial Ostia, MAAR* (1971) 185 ; 172-173. Further on architects' plans, see below p. 30 n. 41.

(32) On the interpretation of *id quod actum est,* see F. Pringsheim, *SZ* 78 (1961) 1-91. Much of this interpretation involved deciding what was done in the absence of explicit contract clauses.

(33) Any ambiguity must be interpreted against the stipulator, see C. Krampe, *SZ* 100 (1983) 185-228 ; H. E. Troye, *SD* 27 (1961) 93-185.

locatio conductio with stipulations providing for payment by the builder to the employer if the project was not completed on time. These stipulations typically offered one of three types of payment :

(1) Stipulations providing for *id quod interest*, the employer's interest money, if the builder defaults (D.19.2.58.1).

(2) Stipulations for *quanti ea res erit*, a payment based roughly upon a calculation of the worth of the object although sometimes extended to include compensation for loss, assessed in the event of the builder's failure to complete the structure (D.45.1.72.1).

(3) Stipulations containing a penalty clause specifying a fixed money payment if the builder defaulted (D.45.1.113 pr.) ([34]).

Stipulations were also used to provide for sureties who pledged themselves to guarantee a contract either of *locatio* or *stipulatio* through *fideiussio* (D.46.1.44 ; 46.3.31) ([35]).

IV. – *Locatio condvctio*

The formation of a valid contract in *locatio conductio* required the parties to agree upon the content of the obligation ; in general, the *locator* placed at the disposal of the *conductor* his thing, his job, or his labor ([36]). Agreement upon a fixed *merces* was also required ([37]). In a contract for construction, the *locator* agreed with the *conductor* upon the nature of the work to be done and furnished the building site. The *conductor* constructed the edifice and received *merces* for his work. In private law sources, the builder is usually referred to as the *conductor*, but also as the *redemptor*. In public contracting, however, the term *redemptor* is more frequently used, both in public building and in other contractual activities let through *locatio conductio* ([38]).

(34) On ancillary stipulations for diversely calculated penalties, including penalty clauses, see below Chapter III, section E.

(35) On arrangements for securing the contract, see below Chapter III, section E.

(36) The most important treatments of *locatio conductio operis* are T. Mayer-Maly, *LC*, and F. M. De Robertis, *I rapporti* 153-177. J. A. C. Thomas, 673-689, and C. A. Cannata, *Colpa* 135-240, discuss many of the sources on construction contracts. For a general introduction to *locatio conductio*, see M. Kaser, *RPR*[2] I 562-572.

(37) The *merces* is also called the *pretium*. This is the major legal requirement for *locatio* : Gaius 3.142 ; D.19.2.2 pr. ; *Inst.* 3.24.

(38) In the private law sources, the terms are used interchangeably ; *redemptor* is the technical term used for contractors in public works. See Festus p. 370M and M. Rostovtsev, *DE* s.v. *conductor*.

The contract was actionable under the *actio locati* or *conducti* respectively, which instructed the *iudex* to decide whether or not the defendant had fulfilled his obligation according to *bona fides* (39).

> *Quod A. Agerius N. Negidio fundum (opus faciendum, operas) quo (quibus) de agitur locauit, qua de re agitur, quidquid ob eam rem N. Negidium A. Agerio dare facere oportet ex fide bona, eius iudex N. Negidium A. Agerio condemnato ; si non paret, absoluito.*

The inclusion of the phrase *ex bona fide* in the formula meant that the performance of the parties was to be judged according to a standard of good faith. The formula instructed the *iudex* to inquire not simply whether the defendant had fulfilled his obligation, but whether he had behaved in good faith in the execution of his duties. The interpretation of the duties and obligations of the parties could take into consideration a broader range of factors beyond the strict promise to perform (40).

As in *stipulatio*, there was no legal requirement that the terms be written, and the existence of a written document specifying contract terms had only evidentiary value. The evidence in the non-legal sources, however, demonstrates clearly that construction projects of any size and complexity were based upon elaborate sets of specifications supplemented by plans and even models. A plan was often procured from an architect as the basis for the specifications (41). Builders could also furnish standard plans from which the employer made a selection (42). The specifications, appended as *leges locationes*, are alluded to in the legal texts. They formed the basis for the employer's approval of the completed structure (D.19.2.24 pr.). As we can see in the *lex parieti faciundo Puteolana*, the well-known public contract for the construction of a wall around the precinct of the temple of Serapis in Puteoli, the clauses contained a detailed description of the precise dimen-

(39) O. Lenel, *EP* 299-300, reconstructs the formula with three hypothetical categories of *locatio*. It is not certain that the Praetor's edict took into account the tripartite division, see M. Kaser, *Iura* 11 (1960) 234 ; H. Kaufmann, 353-359. The *actio conducti* replaced *locauit* with *conduxit*.

(40) In general, see M. Kaser, *RPR*^{2} I 485-488, for bibliography on good faith.

(41) Vitr. 6.8.9-10, defines the architect's main job as furnishing plans ; see also 1.2.2 (types of plans, elevations etc.) ; 1.6.12 and 3.5.8 (drawnings). Cicero often used architects' plans : *Att.* 2.3.2 ; 12.18.1 ; *Q.fr.* 2.2.1 ; 2.5.4. Plut., *Pomp.* 42.4, discusses the sketches Pompey had made of the theatre at Mytilene for his theatre ; *Mor* 498 E speaks about a competition among τεχνῖτοι who bring in models (παραδείγματα).

(42) Gel. 19.10.2 : *Adsistebant fabri aedium complures, balneis nouis moliendis adhibiti, ostendebantque depictas in membranulis uarias species balnearum.*

sions, decoration and structure of the wall (43). Other inscriptions, notably those for road construction, tend to be less specific, mentioning briefly the nature of the work (44). Cato's advice on how to contract for the construction of a villa resembles the contract from Puteoli in the amount and type of detail included. Cato specifies everything including the supply of materials (45).

The process of determining the contract price was a matter of consultation between builder and employer. Labeo alludes to the practice whereby the potential employer commissions the builder to make an estimate, probably in reference to a plan. The estimate formed the basis for the contract price (46). If the employer had consulted an architect to draw the plan, he would already have some notion of the cost of the structure based upon the architect's estimates (47). Ideally, according to Vitruvius, the employer decided the level of expense he wished to maintain, and this was reflected not only in the size and type of the building, but also in the materials and the level of skill. Very often, however, the final cost of completion exceeded the anticipated price (48).

The *merces* could be reckoned in a variety of ways. One method of payment alluded to in the *Digest* seems to have been fairly standard and is further attested both in the contract from Puteoli and in non-legal literary sources : a cost was fixed as a lump sum but was paid out in two installments, one at the beginning of the job, the other after the final approval of the work (49). Costs could also be reckoned in units of measure, a method suitable for jobs involving linear repetition of the same type of work. For example, road construction seems frequently to have been let according to a price-per-foot calculation. Walls and stonework were also well adapted to this sort of pricing (50). The builder's payment was established by measuring

(43) *FIRA* III # 153 = *ILLRP* 518. In general on this inscription, see T. WIEGAND, 660-778.

(44) *ILLRP* 465 = *ILS* 5799, the contract for the paving of the Via Caecilia.

(45) CATO *Agr.* 14.3-15.

(46) LABEO, (*post 5 a Jau. epit.*) D.19.2.60.4.

(47) VITR. 6.8.9-10.

(48) GEL. 19.10.2-4 ; VITR. 10 *praef.* 2 complains about the irresponsibility of architects in allowing cost overrun. VAR., *R.* 3.17.9, tells of Lucius Lucullus who, in his zeal to provide suitable conditions for his fish, lets his architect loose on a spending spree.

(49) *FIRA* III # 153 = *ILLRP* 518. This is implied by LABEO, (*post 5 a Jau. epit.*) D.19.2.60.4. See also FLORENTINUS, (7 *inst.*) D.19.2.36, for lump sum pricing versus a price calculated in units of measure.

(50) The paving of the Via Caecilia (see above note 44) was let in individual contracts which had prices in measurements per foot. R. DUNCAN-JONES, *The Economy of the Roman Empire*[2] (1982) 124-125, hypothesizes that relatively stable calculations per foot underlie

the final product, a process often entrusted to a *mensor aedificiorum* ([51]). Cato calculated the cost of building a new villa according to a fixed price per roof tile ([52]). This price served as a rule of thumb as does, for example, a price per square foot.

In addition to the basic requirements for formation, the parties appended a number of *leges locationis* to the contract to define, alter or increase the contractual duties and requirements. These *leges* are distinct from specifications for the physical aspects of the work. A relatively standardized form of the contract probably came into common use during the Republic, perhaps under the influence of public contracting ([53]). The parties could adapt this contract by adding their own clauses. Many legal texts are concerned with the interpretation of the duties imposed by these terms and clauses.

(1) The *locator* could include a *lex* providing for a fresh contract with a third party should the contractor fail to complete his work on time (D.19.2.13.10). If another contractor were hired because of delay by the first, the employer had an *actio locati* against the first contractor.

(2) Certain clauses defined the final approval of the contract (*probatio*). Usually, the employer himself was named as the approver. But it was probably perfectly normal to include a *lex* naming a third party who was to approve the structure (D.19.2.24 pr.). Presumably, any third party designated by the employer and agreeable to the builder was eligible. One text indicates that the employer could instruct his heir to conduct the approval (D.19.2.60.3).

(3) Separate clauses provided for the hire and payment of specialized, skilled workers, such as stoneworkers (D.19.2.30.3). These jobs were let to *fabri* who probably were hired on the contract of *locatio conductio operarum*.

(4) A completion date was usually set (D.19.2.24 pr. ; 19.2.13.10).

Juristic interpretation of individual cases reveals that the contract was considered to contain two implied terms.

many prices for road construction, but notes various challenges to his interpretations of the relevant inscriptions. On pricing by unit of measure, see FLORENTINUS, D.19.2.36, and ALFENUS, 19.2.30.3.

(51) See COL. 5.1.3 ; PLIN. *Ep.* 10.17b. On the *mensores*, see O. HIRSCHFELD, *Die kaiserlichen Verwaltungsbeamten bis auf Diocletian*[2] (1905, repr. 1975) 267 ; J. P. WALTZING, *Étude historique sur les corporations professionelles chez les Romains* (1895-1900) II 122.

(52) CATO, *Agr.* 14.5.

(53) On *leges locationis*, see V. A. GEORGESCO, *Essai d'une théorie générale des 'leges privatae'* (1932).

(1) Although a completion date was usually included in construction contracts, failure to include this detail did not result in invalidity. In the absence of a specific clause to this effect, the *locator* could bring an action. The jurists instruct the *iudex* to determine whether the builder had exceeded a reasonable time limit. This technique was developed in relationship to the law on *stipulatio* ([54]).

(2) The *locator* could always expect to approve the work and had an action if the quality fell below his expectations according to the specifications. It was common to include a clause defining this procedure, called *probatio.* But in the absence of a clause, the *locator* still was entitled to this inspection of quality (D.19.2.51.1).

The contract of *locatio conductio operis* creates a relationship between the parties based upon the skill of the *conductor* : the *locator* wishes to improve his object, but needs to farm out this job to someone who has the requisite skill for the task. As the early jurists begin to encounter disputes arising from these contracts, their opinions define the liabilities of the parties both in regard to individual aspects of the agreement and in more general terms. The jurists seem particularly interested in isolating the distinguishing characteristics of *locatio conductio operis,* which is perceived as having some similarities to the contract of sale.

Several jurists discuss a typical example of the problems posed by the similarities between the two contracts : if an artisan makes a ring for us, and we pay him for it, is this hire or sale ([55]) ? The basis for distinguishing between the contracts involves determining who supplied the raw material from which the product was made. If the artisan receives the material, works on it and is paid for his work, the contract is hire. If someone simply buys an article already fashioned or, presumably, to be fashioned from the craftsman's material, this is sale. The crucial underlying factor is the jurists' conviction that the balance of interests in hire created in the employer a dependence upon the skill of the artisan. This individual, having received another's object, has the obligation of returning it in improved condition upon completion of the job. The artisan is paid for his skill, and his right to his payment depends upon the employer's acceptance of the work done on the material. The employer has an increased stake in the artisan's skill because he has invested his own material.

(54) See Chapter III, section A.

(55) J. A. C. Thomas, *Mélanges Meylan* I (1963) 339-357, discusses all of the relevant texts ; see further below at note 57.

The jurists had few difficulties in accomodating *locatio conductio* for the construction of a building within this conception of the contract. Four texts deal in particular with the characteristics of building contracts and the builder's responsibility for the building site and for the construction materials.

Pomponius, (9 *ad Sab.*) D.18.1.20

Sabinus respondit, si quam rem nobis fieri uelimus etiam, ueluti statuam uel uas aliquod seu uestem, ut nihil aliud quam pecuniam daremus, emptionem uideri, nec posse ullam locationem esse, ubi corpus ipsum non detur ab eo cui id fieret : aliter atque si aream darem, ubi insulam aedificares, quoniam tunc a me substantia proficiscitur.

The text has been criticized, but seems sound with the exception of *seu uestem*, a possible gloss ([56]). Pomponius records a response by Sabinus who establishes a rule for distinguishing *emptio uendito* from *locatio conductio.* Sabinus' response represents the prevailing view : *locatio* can only exist when the *locator* has furnished the material (*corpus ipsum*) upon which the work will be performed. A money payment for an object made to order will not suffice.

It is obvious that in this circumstance the line dividing sale from hire is thin : an individual desires to obtain an object made to order, such as a statue or a garment. The artisan will have to follow a specific set of instructions and tailor his work according to the buyer's wishes. This arrangement is rather different from a sale from an existing stock of statues or garments. The distinction between sale of an object and hire of the artisan to produce it derives from the source of the material itself. If the artisan has accepted the material from the employer, then the contract is hire. If the artisan produces the object from his own stock, the contract is sale ([57]).

(56) O. LENEL, *Paling.* II 110, considered *seu uestem* an addition by the compilers or a gloss. T. MAYER-MALY, *LC* 74, brackets *etiam* and *seu uestem* ; J. A. C. THOMAS (cited note 55), 341, suspects the classicity of *seu uestem* and, perhaps, the entire last sentence, but in his article on building contracts, 676 n. 10, he seems to accept the last portion as genuine. D. DAUBE, *CJ* 71 (1976) 213-215, offers the most perceptive reading of the text. He translates *etiam* as 'rather', like *immo* or *potius,* and argues that the text as we have it was originally preceded by a statement of transition from an example which contained a clear instance of *emptio uenditio.* Later the text was abbreviated to contain only the more difficult and ambiguous case of an object made to order.

(57) This distinction is elucidated by the jurists in a series of cases devoted to the case of the goldsmith who manufactures a ring from gold. In this instance, *locatio* consisted of a hire accomplished by a payment of money and the transfer of an object to the artisan. But there was not complete agreement among the jurists that the manufacture of a ring by the goldsmith

The last portion of the text applies this line of thought to construction. Sabinus remarks that building presents a distinct situation because the owner furnishes the building site. Thus the *corpus ipsum* is not the material from which the new thing is to be made, a movable, like gold or a cloak, but the contract is still *locatio* because the employer furnishes the land, the essence of what is required for construction. This extends the idea of *locatio operis* as a contract for manufacture out of the *locator*'s goods. The builder is to improve the *locator*'s land through the incorporation of a structure. The implied counter-example would be that we buy a structure built upon land not our own, and this would be sale of both the land and the building.

Paul develops the notion advanced in this text by positing the extreme example of a contract for construction in which the builder is to furnish all of the building material : is this sale of a building or hire of a contractor ?

> Paul, (34 *ad ed.*) D.19.2.22.1-2
>
> *(1) Quotiens autem faciendum aliquid datur, locatio est. (2) Cum insulam aedificandam loco, ut sua impensa conductor omnia faciat, proprietatem quidem eorum ad me transfert et tamen locatio est : locat enim artifex operam suam, id est faciendi necessitatem.*

These two texts have been severely criticized, but it is possible to argue for the soundness of both fragments. In D.19.2.22.1, Paul says that when a job is given to someone to be done, the contract is *locatio*. The expression *aliquid faciendum*, like *opus faciendum*, refers to construction ([58]). This sentence gives a general precept which Paul illustrates in D.19.2.22.2 with the example of a contract specifying that the builder does all the work at his own expense. Property in the building still is transferred to the employer. Ownership of the land is not discussed, but clearly the *locator* was the owner or acted on the owner's behalf. The problem is whether or not the supply of materials affects the nature of the contract.

Mayer-Maly bracketed all of D.19.2.22.1 because it seemed to imply that a contract of *locatio conductio* could be valid without *merces* ([59]). But an examination of the context may mitigate the force of this criticism. Paul is

from his own supply constituted sale. Cassius considered this to be two transactions : *locatio operarum* (GAIUS 3.147) or *operae* (*Inst.* 3.24.5) and *emptio uenditio* of the materials. This view did not prevail. See J. A. C. THOMAS (cited note 55), 340-343, who emends the Gaius text to read *operae* instead of *operarum.* Cf. JAVOLENUS, D.18.1.65, on the production of *tegulae.*

(58) *Opus faciendum* is a standard term for construction jobs, see H. KAUFMANN, 213-219 ; further on *opus*, F. B. J. WUBBE, *TR* 50 (1982) 241-251.

(59) T. MAYER-MALY, *LC* 75. He also considers *locat enim-necessitatem* an interpolation.

not discussing all of the requirements for a valid contract. He rather seeks to establish the characteristics of a construction contract as distinct from the purchase of a new building from the builder. According to his scheme, if the builder supplies the materials for construction, this has no relevance in determining the type of contract. Sabinus' rule in D.18.1.20 underlies this opinion : the ownership of the building site is the crucial element in distinguishing sale from hire.

Paul does not rely entirely upon Sabinus' reasoning but emphasizes another feature which defines the contract as *locatio* : the skill of the contractor who lets out his labor *ut artifex.* The last sentence (*locat enim-necessitatem*) is universally treated as a gloss because the wording suggests day labor (*locatio conductio operarum*). Under this contract, the builder is the *locator* who leases his *operae.* This usage contradicts the explicit reference to *locatio operis* at the beginning of the text ([60]). However, this phrase is not necessarily inherently objectionable. The jurists did not recognize the three categories of *locatio conductio* as separate and defined by fixed terminology. Nor did they discuss any of the three 'types' in reference to each other through the rigid use of names we have come to consider convenient shorthand ([61]). Furthermore, the meaning of the word *opera* in the singular clearly does not mean 'day of work' in this text. The meaning is close to that of *opus,* and *opera* can simply mean 'work'. But *opera* tends to indicate the effort and activity applied to a job rather than the job itself. Paul may have deliberately chosen the more abstract term in order to describe the essence of *locatio,* which he defines as the *artifex* furnishing his skilled labor ([62]).

In the fourth text, Paul cites Labeo's definition of the *opus* :

Paul, (2 *ad ed.*) D.50.16.5.1

'Opere locato conducto' : his uerbis Labeo significari ait id opus, quod Graeci ἀποτέλεσμα uocant, non ἔργον, id est ex opere facto corpus aliquod perfectum.

(60) C. A. CANNATA, *Colpa* 140 n. 1 ; J. A. C. THOMAS, 676. F. B. J. WUBBE (cited note 58), 243, finds this word usage disturbing. He attributes the transfer of ownership in the materials to an implicit sale when it seems clear here and elsewhere that the principle of *superficies solo cedit* accomplishes this, see below, p. 39 and note 71.

(61) M. KASER (cited note 39), 229-234. Cassius' analysis of the contractual arrangement underlying the fabrication of a gold ring from the goldsmith's gold (see note 57 above) is an example of the relative lack of fixed categories and word usage applied *a priori* by the jurists to the discussion of *locatio conductio.*

(62) *Opus* seems to indicate the job or work in a more mechanistic sense while *opera,* particularly in the singular, indicates the effort or professional activity devoted towards a job. Paul's usage may be intended to indicate that under this contract the builder applies his professional services to the *opus.*

This text has never been considered interpolated ([63]). Labeo defines the use of the word *opus* by using two Greek words in order to distinguish his meaning. The distinction between *ἀποτέλεσμα*, full completion, and *ἔργον*, labor or a job, is probably intended to refer to contracts for hire of services as opposed to those for the hire of day labor ([64]). As Wubbe has pointed out, *ἀποτέλεσμα* means full completion or finished product (among other things), whereas *ἔργον* means work, or the object of manufacture ([65]). In using these Greek terms, Labeo defines the contractual obligation of *locatio operis* as encompassing the notion of full completion of a job. *Ἔργον*, however, is simply work without any further implications of control or responsibility. Underlying this distinction is the high degree of control given to the contractor. The job and the site are entrusted to him by reason of his skill. He supervises the work and is responsible for the quality of the finished product.

The concluding phrase (*id est–perfectum*) sums up the results of the comparison by defining the object of the contract as a finished product resulting from the application of the contractor's work. While perhaps unsuited to a definition of all types of work contracts, this is certainly a suitable recapitulation of one aspect of building contracts : the responsibility to create something new and to have total control over it. It seems likely that Labeo arrived at this formulation with construction in mind ([66]).

(63) C. A. CANNATA, *Colpa* 148. F. B. J. WUBBE (cited note 58), 243-247. This is the text upon which L. Amirante based his hypothesis that Labeo was the first to allow the use of *locatio conductio* for manufacture, *Bull.* 62 (1959) 9-119 ; *Labeo* 13 (1967) 49-60 ; Amirante argued for an extremely late emergence of *locatio conductio operis.* He decided that all development of jurisprudence in *locatio conductio* was an enlargement of the "concetto originariamente ristretto di *res locata*". This unifying principle of the contract was that "il conduttore deve assumersi di restituire al locatore la *res locata*". M. KASER (cited note 39), 229-234, has offered the clearest refutation of these views. He defends the authenticity of passages Amirante thought interpolated and criticizes Amirante's methods in general. See also, J. A. C. THOMAS, 674 ; T. MAYER-MALY, *Labeo* 5 (1959) 390-397 ; E. BETTI, *Istituzioni di diritto romano* II i (1960) 219. H. KAUFMANN, 206-219, gives a thorough review of the Republican sources for the contract.

(64) See especially F. M. DE ROBERTIS, *I rapporti*, 154.

(65) F. B. J. WUBBE (cited note 58), 244-246, explores the various meanings of the words in Greek.

(66) F. B. J. WUBBE (cited note 58), 244-247, attempts to demonstrate that this last phrase explains only the word *ἔργον*, and therefore is restricted to defining the physical result of the work. It seems more likely that the *id est* is intended to refer back to the last word of the main clause and recapitulate (in Latin) the conclusion he has demonstrated in the subordinate clause through the use of the Greek words. This reading is not incompatible with Wubbe's assertion (p. 246) that *ἀποτέλεσμα* means "performance accomplie, travail achevé, effort couronné de succès". Labeo's definition *corpus aliquod perfectum* accords perfectly with the

The contractor's responsibility for skill and control is an intrinsic part of *locatio conductio operis* and distinguishes it from other possible arrangements, for example, stipulation or the hire of day labor. Yet the significance of *locatio conductio operis* as a contract for the hire of skilled labor has largely been ignored. Most of the scholarly discussion has concentrated upon reconstructing highly conceptual juristic definitions of the contract, assuming consistent, technical meanings for the terms *opus, opera* and *res* (67). However, these words were not used as technical terms, and we cannot deduce from them the meaning of cases in which they appear.

The object of the contract is much more effectively described in economic terms : *locatio* of a job involved the transfer into the control of the *conductor* an object whose value was improved by his skill. The jurists developed and refined the liabilities in *locatio* as they encountered new cases and factual situations. In contracts for the lease of a job, the liabilities of the contractor grow from the type of skill he is hired to exercise. Generally, the *conductor* is responsible for *imperitia*, a type of *culpa*. A fuller is responsible for his skill and for *custodia*, the safe-keeping of the garments entrusted to him ; the goldsmith or jeweler, for skill in handling a valuable object. The builder must pass *probatio*, an approval process (68). The actual content of the obligation determines to a large degree the pattern of liabilities which emerge from the jurists' law, and to speak of a unified set of rules for *locatio conductio operis* overlooks many of the complexities in the texts.

It is evident from the texts examined earlier that the basis of the contract was the transfer into the builder's control of a plot of land. The arrangements for the supply of materials were evidently left to the parties to decide, and it is conceivable that the builder himself supplied all of the necessary materials as part of his obligation. If this was done, the materials became the

definition 'finished product', and contrasts well with the idea of *ἔργον* as a job, or simply work. Underlying this distinction is the idea of two types of contract, one for full completion, the other for units of work. Wubbe attributes to *ἀποτέλεσμα* an ideal quality as the abstract fulfillment, arguing that a more concrete interpretation would preclude the extension of the 'definition' to other contractual activities like fullery. I think that it is likely, however, that this text was intended to refer to construction. *Opus* is generally used to indicate construction and there is no demonstrable instance of its use to refer to any other type of work contract.

(67) See especially the works of L. AMIRANTE cited above at note 63.

(68) On responsability for *imperitia*, the relevant texts are : ULPIAN, (32 *ad ed.*) D.19.2.13.5 and D.19.2.9.5 (citing Celsus) ; (18 *ad ed.*) D.9.2.27.29. See below Chapter III, section B, on *periculum* and the liabilities of the parties. On *probatio*, see below Chapter III, section C.

property of the landowner as they were built into the structure on the principle of *superficies solo cedit*:

> Ulpian, (17 *ad ed.*) D.6.1.39
>
> *Redemptores, qui suis cementis aedificant, statim cementa faciunt eorum, in quorum solo aedificant.*

The text is generally considered to be free of interpolation ([69]). Materials belonging to the contractor and used in construction become the property of the owner of the soil. J. P. Meincke observed that while the *iusta causa* of the passage of ownership is actually the contract, the change of ownership itself proceeds from the rule *superficies solo cedit* ([70]). The existence of this principle allowed the jurists to establish the site as the substance of the contract. Certainly a building contract undertaken on mandate for the landowner by an associate would result in ownership of the materials by the landowner and not by the contracting party. Provisions for the supply of materials were sure to have been made in the contract. The *merces* would have been calculated either to include or exclude expenditures for materials ([71]).

Even though the cost and procurement of the materials is of secondary importance in the juristic discussion, there is no doubt that this aspect of the construction required a great deal of effort, planning and money. Cato's sample contract contains a number of specific instructions concerning the materials. The employer supplies all of the materials and some tools ([72]). This may have been common practice. The contract from Puteoli contains no references to the supply of materials, but does specify that certain materials, such as iron and wood, should be used ([73]).

According to Cato, the builder was to finish the materials which he had to integrate into the construction, for example, hewing and smoothing logs or preparing stone. He could also be responsible for supplying the materials, as the juristic sources cited above indicate. Alfenus (D.19.2.30.3) refers to

(69) The only criticism is that of G. Beseler, *Beiträge* III 2-3, who preferred to read <*non*> *statim. Contra*: A. Guarneri-Citati, *APal.* 14 (1930) 347 n. 3, who points out that it is absurd to imagine that a builder who has paid for materials and received reimbursement in the form of *merces* should remain the owner of the materials.

(70) J. P. Meincke, *SZ* 88 (1971) 152.

(71) A. Guarneri-Citati (cited note 69), 347, affirms the contractual basis of the transfer of the ownership of the materials; so too, M. Kaser, *SZ* 65 (1947) 234 n. 49. Cf. F. B. J. Wubbe (cited note 58), 243.

(72) Cato, *Agr.* 14. See bibliography cited above at note 6.

(73) *FIRA* III # 153 = *ILLRP* 518.

a *lex locationis* providing for stonework with a price calculated to include the cost of the stone as well as the labor. Ulpian (D.6.1.39, cited above) speaks of a builder supplying the *cementa.* And so perhaps many of the common, everyday items for construction were procured by the builder. His primary responsibility for skill encompassed the proper handling of the basic materials required for the fabrication of the building, and he would be liable for damage done to them in the process of building ([74]). Typical materials would be wood and stone, widely used in domestic structures of all types. Walls were frequently made of *opus caementicium,* consisting of *pozzolana,* aggregate and material for facing the concrete. Rome was very well supplied with many of the natural materials required and also had markets where both builders and employers could purchase the necessary supplies.

If the employer wished to incorporate expensive or rare materials into the structure, he often procured them himself or through an intermediary. Pliny, in his letter to Mustius, wrote about the restoration of a temple on one of his properties. Although Mustius' field of expertise is not mentioned, he furnishes the plan for the restoration project and is probably trained as an architect. Pliny also puts Mustius in charge of obtaining four marble columns and other marble and leaves the selection to him ([75]). In a letter to Atticus, Cicero expresses concern about procuring special materials and mentions that he has instructed Apella of Chios to acquire marble columns and pillars ([76]). An interesting parallel is afforded by references in both Vitruvius and Pliny to wall painting. The decoration of walls was let to a separate specialist on contract ([77]). In general, the painter supplied the colors. When the employer desired especially bright colors, an expensive commodity, he tended to omit these from the specifications of the painter's contract and supply them himself ([78]). No reason is given for this practice which both authors consider to be standard. Evidently, the painter of walls was not expected to keep in his stock expensive and precious colors.

(74) The builder would doubtless be responsible for damage to the materials in handling them, although no legal texts deal specifically with this topic. An interesting text, although it involves a contract for the transport of columns, is GAIUS, (10 *ad ed. prou.*) D.19.2.25.7. A *conductor* has undertaken to transport columns, and they have been broken during transportation. He is responsible for any damage and also for the activities of his employees who may have mishandled the columns. However, he is not responsible if he behaved as diligently as possible. M. KASER, *RPR*[2] I 571 n. 86.

(75) PLINY, *Ep.* 9.39.

(76) CICERO, *Att.* 12.19.1.

(77) PAUL, (5 *quaest.*) D.19.5.5.2.

(78) PLINY, *Nat.* 35.30 ; 35.44 ; VITR., 7.5.8.

V. – *STIPVLATIO* AND *LOCATIO CONDVCTIO*

As we have seen, the two types of contracts commonly used for the purposes of construction differed substantially in the type of obligation they furnished. Both were generally used to employ a contractor for the construction of an entire building, but the characteristics of each type resulted in agreements which differed substantially in content and in liabilities. In *stipulatio,* the obligation was summed up in a promise, and the subsequent fulfillment by the builder was judged largely in terms of his adherence to a relatively circumscribed agreement. The jurists are reluctant to infer from the words of the promise very many implied terms. There is no juristic discussion of the degree of skill the builder was intended to bring to the contract ; there is no mention of an approval process. The interpretation of the contract, insofar as it can be reconstructed, remains relatively firmly rooted in the few basic requirements for validity, and questions of performance are assessed in terms of delayed or timely completion. Indeed, stipulation may have been ideal for a landowner who was less concerned with advance guarantees of the skill of the worker and more anxious to provide for the completion of the structure to term.

Locatio conductio created a relationship based upon reliance and good faith. The initial agreement is more detailed than a typical *stipulatio* both in express clauses and in implied terms. The builder is hired not just as a construction expert, although this skill is assumed, but also for his expertise in coordinating the project. He is expected to procure some of the materials and labor force (D.19.2.30.3). He is also required to submit his work to a final approval process. Although the building may not be large, he is put entirely in charge of it. The juristic interpretation of the contractual obligations assumes that the parties have certain implicit duties and liabilities created by the formation of the contract, such as the responsibility for harm to the building site or for faulty work. Many of these implicit duties were established and defined through the opinions of the jurists, as we will see in Chapter III. In the following chapter, however, we will examine the building scene at Rome to see how these two contracts fit into a larger pattern of organization of building projects.

CHAPTER II

The Organization of Private Building at Rome

Contracting for the completion of a whole building, although doubtless a popular way of hiring skilled workers, was not the only method of organizing Roman construction projects. In this chapter, our concern will be to identify how individuals interested in building for private use matched their need for labor with the available pool of construction workers, and how these workers were organized to carry out the work (1). The economy of private building in Roman antiquity encompassed several typical organizational patterns, and the choice of method depended to a large extent upon the capacity of the employer for organization and supervision. Because building tends to be a slow, labor-intensive enterprise which requires skilled workers, the decision to contract with a builder for the completion of a whole job offered certain advantages to the landowner, particularly if he wished simply to place the entire organizational responsibility for the job in the charge of one person. This pattern of contracting created a relatively detached and short-term relationship with the builder and was particularly convenient for the person who built infrequently or had no ready source of skilled workers.

But different needs and the composition of the labor force at Rome provided other possible methods of obtaining trained builders. Trained slaves were an important source of skilled work either within the master's *familia* or on hire or loan to another (2). Of course, the status of slaves as property

(1) The following studies of construction in other societies have offered helpful insights into the nature of construction as an enterprise : A. Burford, *The Greek Temple Builders at Epidauros* (1969) ; P. J. Cassimatis, "The Economics of the Construction Industry" in *Studies in Business Economics* 111 (1969) ; E. W. Cooney, *Economic History Review* 8 (1955-56) 167-176 and *Architectural Research and Teaching* 1 (1970) 46-52 ; H. J. Dyos, *Victorian Studies* 11 (1967-68) 641-690 ; R. Goldthwaite, *The Building of Renaissance Florence* (1980) esp. 115-119.

(2) On the use of slaves and freedmen, see especially below at section III. Ulpian, (28 *ad ed.*) D.13.6.5.7, mentions the loan of a slave *tector*.

meant that the mechanisms of their employment tended to be out of the purview of the legal system. Independent builders, both freeborn and freed, were also hired to work on small segments of a project on a daily basis through the contract of *locatio conductio operarum.* Our knowledge of contracting for day laborers is circumscribed by the lack of evidence in the legal sources, but it seems that day laborers were often used as supplementary workers hired by a principal contractor. A landowner could also choose to organize a job in a series of smaller contracts, and presumably either *locatio* or *stipulatio* could be used to hire a builder for a portion of a larger project ([3]). Any of these methods of organization placed upon the employer a large supervisory role and greater control over the project during the actual process of building.

Since our concern is with the employment of skilled laborers who are essential to any complex construction project, almost no attention will be given here to the problems associated with the supply and use of unskilled labor. Generally, unskilled workers were acquired from whatever source of manpower was available in proportion to the size of the job ([4]). We hear that 30,000 men were continuously at work on Claudius' project to build an emissary from the Fucine lake. Nero pressed convicts into service in order to build a channel from Misenum to Lake Avernus ([5]). The need for labor of this sort, used primarily to move earth or do other heavy tasks, is characteristic of imperial projects of great size, rather than the smaller private projects with which we are concerned.

The main goal of this chapter will be to suggest favored patterns of organization in Roman construction, principally as they are attested in non-legal sources. The legal sources are particularly informative about the legal disputes of contractors, but they tell us little about the larger context of the building trade. The great abundance of physical evidence for the

(3) Hire of labor by the day, *locatio conductio operarum,* is notoriously underrepresented in the *Digest,* see F. M. DE ROBERTIS, *I rapporti* 127-152, and M. KASER, *RPR*[2] I 568-570. According to A. BURFORD (cited note 1), 110-111, the extensive hire of day laborers preceded the use of contractors as a method of organizing the construction of temples in fifth century Athens.

(4) On the hire of urban poor as a source of labor for public building projects in the Empire, see P. A. BRUNT, *JRS* 70 (1980) 81-100. For another view, L. CASSON, *Ancient Trade and Society* (1984) 122-125, restates his earlier objections to Brunt's interpretation of SUET. *Ves.* 18 as implying the hire of free poor in public works.

(5) On the labor supply necessary to build an outlet from the Fucine lake, SUET. *Cl.* 20.3. On corvées of prisoners, see SUET. *Nero* 31.3 (Avernus) ; *Nero* 19 and JOSEPHUS, *BJ* 3.540 (Corinth). R. MACMULLEN, *HSPh* 64 (1959) 207-235.

building activities of the Romans, particularly in ancient Ostia, places before our eyes the final result of the development of the land by construction for private use. But most of the steps in this process are missing, so that little can be said about patterns of property ownership, financial arrangements for building, and the size and organization of construction. The state of the evidence rules out any thorough studies of the configuration of the building industry which are available for other societies and thwarts any attempts at ascertaining, for example, what percentage of building was undertaken on contract, what the typical size of projects was, whether or not there were companies of builders and how many builders were slaves, freedmen or free born ([6]). Despite these limitations, certain organizational patterns do emerge, and when viewed along with the information available from the *Digest*, suggest the growth of a prosperous, diversely constituted, building trade in the first centuries of the Empire.

I. – The Employers

It seems worthwhile to begin by considering how landowners and potential employers of builders approached the organization of new construction projects. The initial stages in the process, for example, decisions about the plans, the appropriate level of expense and the acquisition of skilled labor, would depend upon the size and purpose of the construction. In general, the need for new construction extended to several different types of projects, and the *Digest* texts refer to houses (*domus*), villas and *insulae* as typical of those structures let on contract to builders ; one text mentions the construction of a *riuus* ([7]). Some families had extensive and long-term interests in building as did, for example, the Statilii Tauri, a family rising to prominence under Augustus. Among their family holdings were *horti* and an amphitheatre ([8]).

(6) Cf. the information available concerning Greek temple construction, A. Burford (cited note 1), chapters 4-7. Studies of the organization of Roman construction are few : on public building in the Empire, see P. A. Brunt (cited note 4), 81-100 ; an earlier treatment is in H. Loane, *Industry and Commerce in the City of Rome* (1938) 79-86. The most complete study of Roman building by far is the dissertation of J. L. D. Pearse. On imperial building in the provinces, see R. MacMullen (cited note 5), 207-235.

(7) Typical examples are D.19.2.22.2 (*insulam aedificandam*) ; D.19.2.59 (*domum faciendam*) ; D.19.2.60.4 (*uillam aedificare*). On cases in *stipulatio*, see Chapter I n. 29. Labeo, (1 *pith.*) D.19.2.62, refers to the construction of a *riuus*. The construction of *monumenta* is discussed below at pages 48-49 and note 20.

(8) On this family and their building interests, see below pages 64-65 and notes 92-96.

But members of the Roman upper classes, who were most likely to acquire, develop and dispose of property, probably engaged in building projects belonging to one of four broad categories : residential housing (both in the city and in the country), funerary monuments, property for commercial exploitation (*insulae, tabernae*) and maintenance, service or repair work.

Cicero's property holdings and building activity exemplify a common pattern of property development among the upper classes. He bought property and engaged both in construction of new residences and in the improvement of the preexisting structures ([9]). Cicero had several pieces of rental property and from time to time arranged for their upkeep and maintenance ([10]). He supervised the refurbishment or remodeling of his brother's property both in Rome and in the countryside while Quintus was in Sardinia and in Gaul ([11]). One building project in particular was especially dear to Cicero : the fane he envisaged for his daughter Tullia after her death. Cicero's search for an appropriate site for Tullia's fane demonstrates how difficult and costly acquisition of property could be. He entered into negotiations with a number of potential vendors and was finally unable to procure the proper *horti* ([12]). Cicero's preoccupation with his property as a sign of status and a mode of self expression was shared by many wealthy Roman landowners. Typically, he also was disinclined to attend personally to the maintenance or management of his rental property and relied upon dependents or middlemen ([13]).

While Cicero provides an example of individual development of property for personal use, other, more speculative, patterns of property development by building are attested in the Republic. C. Sergius Orata, in league with a physician, Asclepiades of Prusa, bought properties, furnished them with

(9) On Cicero's property, I. SHATZMAN, *Senatorial Wealth and Roman Politics* (1975) 403-409 (Cicero) and 425-427 (Quintus) ; E. RAWSON, in *Studies in Roman Property* (ed. M. I. FINLEY, 1976) 85-102.

(10) CICERO owned *insulae* on the Argiletum and Aventine in Rome (*Att.* 12.32.2) and a portion of another (*Att.* 15.26.4). In Puteoli he had *tabernae* (*Att.* 13.45.2-3 ; 13.46.3) ; after the collapse of these buildings, Cicero sent Chrysippus to inspect them (*Att.* 14.9.1 and below page 50). On Cicero's rental property, B. W. FRIER, *CJ* 74 (1978) 1-6 and *LTIR* chapter 2.

(11) Repairs to the house in Rome : *Q.fr.* 2.4.2 ; on Marcus' supervision of the property at Arpinum : *Q.fr.* 3.1.1-2.

(12) D. R. SHACKLETON BAILEY, *Cicero's Letters to Atticus* V (1966) 404-413, reconstructs Cicero's plans for the fane and in particular his unsuccessful search for a suitable piece of property upon which to build it. On high land costs at Rome, see R. DUNCAN-JONES, *PBSR* 33 (1965) 177-188.

(13) See B. W. FRIER (cited note 10), 4-5, and *LTIR* chapter 2. Cicero's primary interest is in the income.

balneae pensiles and resold them ([14]). Large-scale speculation in land for development (and possible resale) has been hypothesized on the basis of Plutarch's reference to Crassus' veritable army of 500 servile builders and architects. Crassus is said to have bought up property cheaply from owners after fires, presumably in order to rebuild quickly and gain a profit by reselling the refurbished plots. If this was his scheme, it is the only explicit example of large-scale building for speculative purposes. The practice of maintaining a force of building specialists, especially for speculative purposes, was apparently not common ([15]). The cost would be very high, and one could not always count on a continuous demand to justify the expense.

Although there is little literary evidence for patterns of property exploitation in the Empire, much building for private use doubtless remained in the hands of the upper ranks of society. One example is the younger Pliny, who bought homes and villas for private use and then improved them according to his own taste ([16]). He was, however, not known to possess any urban commercial property. As for major construction projects of the first two centuries of the Empire, such as the rebuilding of Rome after the fire of 64 and the new building at Ostia, no sources reveal to us the concerns and identities of those who were constructing dwellings for private use. At Ostia, many private individuals built primarily for their own needs, and these projects included both homes and commercial property such as the will of Iunia Libertas records in the mid-second century A.D. ([17]). Other complexes were built for investment as rental property. Examples of this phenomenon

(14) On the activities of Orata, see E. RAWSON (cited note 9), 100-101. He was active in the nineties B.C., see PLINY, *Nat.* 9.168 ; F. MÜNZER, *RE* s.v. Sergius (Orata) # 33 col. 1713-1714 (1923).

(15) Plutarch, *Crassus* 2.4-5. On this anecdote, H. LOANE (cited note 6), 81-82, citing H. GUMMERUS, *Klio* 16 (1920) 190-192, assumed that Crassus' interest was in quick rebuilding and resale. This text is somewhat difficult to interpret, but offers evidence for the large-scale use by a private individual of slave builders and architects. It should be treated with caution because of the anomalous nature of the episode. Even families with established building interests had far fewer slaves in the *familia* trained as builders. See below on the Statilii Tauri, and J. L. D. PEARSE, 66, on the numbers of trained builders attested epigraphically (see further at notes 81 and 92).

(16) R. DUNCAN-JONES, *The Economy of the Roman Empire*[2] (1982) 22-24. Pliny had a hand in much building and remodeling, but tells us almost nothing about his own methods of carrying out building : *Ep.* 2.17 ; 5.6 ; 9.7. Pliny was typical of wealthy Romans in that he also spent a large amount of money on donations for public building.

(17) See R. MEIGGS, *Roman Ostia*[2] (1973) 68-69. Much of the building in Ostia, apart from that sponsored or financed by the government, seems to have been undertaken by private individuals or entities such as *collegia*, see MEIGGS, 76, and F. WILSON, *PBSR* 13 (1935) 41-68.

are the Casette-Tipo complex, which is Trajanic, and the Garden Houses, built during the reign of Hadrian ([18]). *Collegia* also owned and developed property ; the *fabri tignarii* of Ostia built their *schola* on a large plot adjacent to the forum and had other important property holdings near the center of town ([19]).

There were, presumably, some small businesses devoted to land development. Ulpian, in D.17.2.52.7, discusses a partnership formed between two individuals for the purpose of developing small parcels of land for resale as *monumenta.* They pooled their financial resources and expertise : Flavius Victor furnished the money for the purchase of the land and for the materials ; Bellicus Asianus supplied the labor and expertise (*opera et peritia*) and constructed the *monumenta.* The finished product was then sold separately in parcels to buyers ([20]). The text implies that there were numerous monuments being built. After the initial investment in this small-scale construction project, Flavius Victor received a fixed portion of the profit. He could expect a fairly safe return and had none of the bother of the construction. Asianus kept any money remaining after this payment. The amount of Asianus' income would depend upon his success at keeping costs down and charging enough for the monuments. He presumably directed a workshop specializing in stone work and sculpture. This small company

(18) R. Meiggs (cited note 17), 134, on the Cassette Tipo (III.xii-xiii) ; 76 and 139, on the Garden Houses (III.ix).

(19) On the guild property near the forum, the Casa dei Triclini (I.xii), see G. Hermansen, *Ostia, Aspects of Roman City Life* (1981) 62-63 and 96-111. The *collegium* also owned property at the corner of the Decumanus and Via degli Augustales, R. Meiggs (cited note 17), 595. Hermansen would add the Casseggiato del Temistocle to their holdings.

(20) Ulpian, (31 *ad ed.*) D.17.2.52.7, citing Papinian :

> *Item ex facto consultum respondisse se ait libro tertio responsorum : inter Flauium Victorem et Bellicum Asianum placuerat, ut locis emptis pecunia Victoris monumenta fierent opera et peritia Asiani, quibus distractis pecuniam Victor cum certa quantitate reciperet, superfluum Asianus acciperet, qui operam in societatem contulit : erit pro socio actio.*

J. Crook, *Law and Life of Rome* (1967) 230, interprets this arrangement as a partnership between an architect and a land agent ; I. Calabi-Limentani, *Studi sulla società romana* (1958) 76, includes this passage under her discussion of sculptors, and considers Asianus either a sculptor or an architect. The reference to *peritia* and the fact that Asianus and his workers apparently design, build and decorate the monuments indicate that Asianus was a builder who had a workshop of stoneworkers, including some with expertise in sculpting. An interesting parallel is furnished by the activities of the Haterii, who built their own monument, perhaps using sculptors in their *familia* or those customarily in their employ for work on other monuments, see F. Coarelli, in *Studies in Classical Art and Archaeology. A tribute to Peter Heinrich von Blanckenhagen* (edd. G. Kopcke and M. B. Moore, 1979) 255-269. Similarly employed was the fictional freedman Habinnas, a friend of Trimalchio, and a *lapidarius* who made *monumenta* (Petr. 65.5 ; 71.5-12).

suggests that there were other such businesses specializing in the construction of small structures such as *monumenta.*

In the early stages of a construction project, the landowner had to consider what sort of plan he desired for the building and may, therefore, have consulted an architect. Architects were an important source of expertise for the landowner, who probably had little experience in design, and it is an unusual feature of Roman building that so little is known about the methods typically used to engage their services. Since their skill did not involve manufacture, they were not hired on *locatio conductio operis* ([21]). Architects were qualified to design rather than build structures and received technical and artistic training. They may have been hired in the same way as *mensores,* whose skill was also technical rather than manual. As we know from Ulpian in D.11.6.1 pr., *mensores* were generally engaged on the contract of mandate, which meant that they received an *honorarium* instead of a wage. He cites the opinion of the early jurists that *mensores* should not be hired for a daily fee through *locatio conductio operarum* because of their superior skill. But as another text shows, they did occasionally engage their services for a daily wage, and so both means of hire were probably common ([22]). Although Columella (5.1.3) points out that architects disdained to do the job of measurers, the two skills may have merited the same sort of legal consideration.

According to Vitruvius, the architect guided the owner through the construction, first supplying the plans and then helping in the formation of the contract. Vitruvius suggests that the architect should acquire a knowledge of the law, so that he can counsel the parties during the formulation of the contract clauses. The skillful composition of the clauses could spare both parties legal problems during the term of the contract ([23]). It is conceivable

(21) On the job of architects, see also above at Chapter I. They were designers, not builders, and no *Digest* text links them with *locatio operis,* despite misconceptions in the scholarship on this point. See especially K. VISKY, *IURA* 10 (1959) 53-66, and R. DÜLL, *SZ* 69 (1952) 420-427, who assumed that the texts in D.19.2 refer to the employment of architects.

(22) ULPIAN, (24 *ad ed.*) D.11.6.1 pr. On the contract of mandate, see M. KASER, *RPR*[2] I 569 ; 577-580. ULPIAN, D.11.6.1.1, and PAUL, (23 *ad ed.*) D.10.1.4.1, imply that *mensores* accept daily wages. Under Septimius Severus, architects and *redemptores* could be sued under the *actio si mensor falsum modum dixerit,* see D.11.6.7.3.

(23) VITR. 1.1.10 :

> *Item, aquarum ductiones et cetera, quae eius modi sunt, nota oportet sint architectis, uti ante caueant quam instituant aedificia, ne controuersiae factis operibus patribus familiarum relinquantur, et ut legibus scribendis prudentia cauere possit et locatori et conductori ; namque si lex perite fuerit scripta, erit ut sine captione uterque ab utroque liberetur.*

that the architect continued to advise the landowner throughout the period of construction and either conducted the final approval himself or aided the employer in this process ([24]).

Cicero made use of several architects in his building projects. They designed new buildings, supervised repairs and gave advice on the purchase of pre-existing structures. Among the names frequently mentioned were those of Cyrus and his freedman Vettius Chrysippus ([25]). Cicero was on good terms with both men and was (along with Clodius) Cyrus' heir. Chrysippus presumably learned his skill as a slave and was a freedman at the time of Cyrus' death in 52. He continued to work for Cicero.

Cicero consulted both men frequently for designs and mentions in particular Cyrus' plan for some windows (*Att.* 2.3.2). He summoned either Cyrus or Chrysippus to help in repair work when the wall of the palaestra in the house on the Palatine threatened to collapse into Quintus' property ([26]). On another occasion, Chrysippus was dispatched to Puteoli when two of Cicero's *tabernae* required repairs. He was to undertake an estimate of the necessary work and was aided by Cicero's businessman Vestorius (*Att.* 14.9.1). Chrysippus also inspected a parcel of land, a suburban estate with a villa, for potential use as the site of Tullia's fane ([27]).

Cicero had occasion to employ other architects on his building projects. He mentions a certain Cluatius, who submitted a plan for Tullia's fane ([28]). He also refers in passing to Corumbus, a slave of his friend Balbus, who had been summoned to the Tusculan villa in the midst of a building project in

(24) PAUL (D.19.2.24 pr.) and LABEO (D.19.2.60.3) both indicate that any third party could be chosen as approver. See also CIC. *Q.fr.* 3.1.2, where Caesius is supervising (*curat*) Diphilus (probably a *conductor*). Caesius may be an architect or *uilicus*, see below, p. 54 and note 48.

(25) CICERO considered architecture *honesta* for those who needed to work (*Off.* 1.151) and thought it was a false economy to omit consultation with an architect (*N.D.* 1.72). On Cyrus, at work between 60 and 56 B.C., *Att.* 2.3.2 ; *Q.fr.* 2.2.2 ; on his death in 52, *Mil.* 46. S. TREGGIARI, *Roman Freedmen during the late Republic* (1969) 134, thinks he was a freedman or enfranchised alien ; J. L. D. PEARSE, 16-17 ; 21-22, thinks Cyrus' name and status indicate that he was a freedman. D. R. SHACKLETON BAILEY (cited note 12), I (1965), on *Att.* 2.3.2, derives Cyrus' *nomen*, Vettius, from that of his freedman, Vettius Chrysippus. On Chrysippus' activities, see *Att.* 14.9.1 ; *Att.* 13.29.1 ; *Fam.* 7.14.1 and J. L. D. PEARSE, 21-22.

(26) *Att.* 2.4.7 : Cicero summons Vettius.

(27) On the *tabernae*, *Att.* 14.9.1. On the *horti Scapulani*, *Att.* 13.29.1 ; D. R. SHACKLETON BAILEY (cited note 12), V 410-412, gives an account of this and other letters concerning the fane.

(28) *Att.* 12.18.1 ; 12.36.2. Cluatius is not specifically called *architectus*.

44 ([29]). Finally, we hear of Numisius who had made a *forma*, or architectural plan, for Quintus ([30]).

As we can see, Cicero had at his disposal a number of architects of differing status, slaves, freedmen and freeborn individuals, most of whom worked independently in their profession. They were not members of his *familia* or dependent upon him in any way except for the wage or honorarium he must have paid. This group is representative of the small number of architects whose identity is known to us. Many were freedmen, trained as slaves, then continuing as architects upon manumission ([31]). Not all architects worked autonomously as practitioners. Some worked together with builders and designed standardized plans from which the potential employer could select the most suitable ([32]). Alternatively, some architects may have also worked as *redemptores*, which would be a way of hedging against the instability of the building trade ([33]). There were also families whose members seem to produce both architects and builders, as, for example, P. Cornelius Architectus, whose *cognomen* may represent his skill, and his son, P. Cornelius Thallus, *magister quinquennalis* of the *collegium fabrum tignariorum* of Rome. For these men, construction seems to be a family enterprise ([34]). Thus, although the architect's job qualified him to work in all aspects of the building process, often, when functioning as a designer, he

(29) *Att.* 14.3.1 : *Corumbus Balbi nullus adhuc. est mihi notum nomen ; bellus enim esse dicitur architectus.*

(30) *Q.fr.* 2.2.1 J. L. D. PEARSE, 18, thinks he is *ingenuus.* In *Fam.* 7.20.1, Cicero mentions a Rufio in connection with building done in 44. D. R. SHACKLETON BAILEY, *Cicero : Epistulae ad Familiares* II (1977) 473 identifies this Rufio as a slave or freedman of Trebatius, the addressee, and connects him to C. Trebatius Rufio, mentioned in *CIL* VI 16120 as aiding in the erection of a monument to a Q. Cornelius. His participation is supervisory : *faciendum curauerunt ex testamento eius.* Perhaps he was trained as an architect.

(31) J. L. D. PEARSE, chapter 4 and Appendix B, gives the most complete list of individuals who can be identified as architects. More than half of the architects from Rome and Italy were slaves or freedmen. On their relatively humble condition in relationship to other buiders, see P. GROS, in *Architecture et Société, Collection de l'École Française de Rome* 66 (1983) 431-432.

(32) GEL. 19.10.1-4.

(33) See below at pages 57-58 on L. Cocceius who may have been both *redemptor* and architect.

(34) On P. Cornelius Thallus, son of Architectus, see *CIL* VI 148 = XIV 5 ; *CIL* VI 30703 and 10299. The grandson, P. Cornelius Architectianus, was a member of the *ordo decurionum* probably at Ostia. On the *cognomen*, which surely also refers to his skill, see H. GUMMERUS, in *Commentationes philologicae in honorem Professoris Emeriti I. A. Heikel* (1926) 63. On Thallus' membership in the Roman *collegium*, see J. MORE, *The Fabri Tignarii of Rome* (diss. Harvard, 1969) chapter 1 ; this view is supported by the recent observations of S. PANCIERA, *ZPE* (1981) 271-280, and J. L. D. PEARSE, *Epigraphica* 37 (1975) 100-123.

worked on the side of the employer as his consultant and perhaps supervised in his behalf. However, as we will see, it is possible that architects also sought employment as part of building companies.

II. – Builders Hired on Contract

Very little non-legal evidence survives to tell the story of the lives and careers of typical Roman builders. Most of the sources are brief epigraphic references, either funerary inscriptions or inscriptions dealing with the activities of the *collegium fabrum tignariorum*, containing no more than names and offering no further clues to the employment and livelihood of the individuals involved. A further difficulty is posed by the number of different terms in Latin which may refer to skilled builders. The most common are *faber, faber intestinarius, faber tignarius, structor, structor parietarius, constructor, tector*, in addition to other workers who specialized in working with individual materials ([35]). None of these terms indicates either how these people were employed or the degree of control they exercised over a project. Some were contractors, but many worked as slaves or freedmen within a *familia*; others were small-scale employees of builders.

In non-legal sources, the only terms which indicate how a builder was employed are those used to designate a builder hired on contract, *conductor* or *redemptor*, the latter being much more frequently used. Alternatively, word usage such as *locauit* or *conduxit faciendum* can indicate a contractual situation ([36]). Because this is the only mode of organization which can be described from literary sources, it is best to begin with an account of the hire, organization and identity of contractors in the late Republic and early Empire.

Most of the evidence for the use of contractors comes from the Republic when contracting was the standard way of building new public monuments and works and maintaining those already in existence ([37]). Contracting was generally used to farm out many other vital services, such as tax collec-

(35) See further on these titles below at section III and at note 81.

(36) On the epigraphical evidence for *redemptores*, see A. Biscardi, *DE* s.v. *locatio*; on *conductores*, M. Rostovtsev, *DE* s.v. *conductor*. The former was the technical term for public contractor. The latter is more frequently used in private law sources. The *Thesaurus Linguae Latinae* kindly provided me with references to *redemptores*.

(37) In general on the administration of public building during this period, see D. E. Strong, *Bull. Inst. Class. Stud.* 15 (1968) 97-109. See above at Chapter I on the similarities between the forms of contracts used in public and private contracting.

tion ([38]). As we have seen, the general procedure is relatively clear, and the form of these contracts was similar to that in private *locatio* as the contract from Puteoli suggests. Although the contractors themselves are often referred to simply as *redemptores*, some are known by name. C. Blossius, the *redemptor* of the Puteolan contract, was probably attached to a prosperous family in the south and may have been a person of some substance because he seems to have pledged property to guarantee the contract ([39]). P. Iunius, the *redemptor* for the maintenance of the temple of Castor, was a relatively humble person himself in terms of status. But he had the support of his patron, D. Brutus, and was associated with other *redemptores* some of whom were of equestrian rank ([40]). These *redemptores* organized the work, but it is impossible to ascertain whether they themselves had any practical training in building. They were, in any case, responsible for demonstrating the quality of the work in an approval process. Perhaps *fabri* were hired to do the actual construction work ([41]).

Much of the non-legal testimony for builders at work in the Republic mirrors the model we find in the legal sources. Cato discusses the preferred method of hiring a builder to construct a villa. The builder (*faber*) is under contract for the whole job, and the text describes the work in detailed specifications ([42]). Cato does not mention whether the builder is working alone or with other workers. In 56 B.C., Cicero writes twice to his brother in Sardinia concerning repairs to Quintus' house on the Palatine. He first refers simply to the *redemptor* to whom he has made a payment of one half the contract price ([43]). The contractor seems to be working in conjunction with *fabri*. Cicero's adjacent house is also being repaired, and he boasts that he is simultaneously building on three sites and remodeling his other houses. He admits that this is a costly venture, but seems to feel that this is warranted in order to enhance his post-exile image (*Q.fr.* 2.5.1). Soon after this, Cicero

(38) E. Badian, *Publicans and Sinners* (1972) ; P. Garnsey in *Trade in the Ancient Economy* (edd. P. Garnsey, K. Hopkins, C. R. Whittaker, 1983) 118-130.

(39) On C. Blossius, see below at Chapter III, section E.

(40) On P. Iunius, see below at Chapter III, section E.

(41) Implied in Cic. 2 *Verr.* i.147.

(42) Cato, *Agr.* 14 : *Villam aedificandam si locabis nouam ab solo, faber haec faciat oportet.* The builder is later called *conductor.* On this passage, P. Thielscher, *Des Marcus Cato Belehrung über die Landwirtschaft* (1963) 222-223, rejects the idea that this is a contract of hire ; but see H. Kaufmann, 24 and 222.

(43) *Q.fr.* 2.4.2 : *Redemptori tuo dimidium pecuniae curaui.* This is standard practice when a contract price is fixed in a lump sum, see above at Chapter I and below at Chapter III, section D.

reports to Quintus that the building is progressing well : *Res agebatur multis structoribus. Longilium redemptorem cohortatus sum* (44). The contractor, a certain Longilius, is working along with many builders and, Cicero says, has given his assurances of his eagerness to please. The builders are working from a *forma*, perhaps drawn by Cyrus. The work on Quintus' house seems still to be in progress two years later when Cicero alludes to *redemptores* who are working on plastering and finishing work (*expolitiones*) (45).

Cicero's letter to his brother in September of 54 is full of news concerning the building projects which Cicero has again been supervising in Quintus' absence. Cicero makes a tour of the Manilian property, one of his brother's estates in Arpinum, where extensive work is underway. Either an entire villa is being built, or an existing one is undergoing remodeling with substantial additions. The builder in charge, Diphilus, receives special mention because of his slowness (46). Cicero refers to a bath, promenade and aviary as still to be done ; finishing touches are being applied to the villa itself. Cicero's tour amounts to an interim *probatio*, and he finds fault with certain aspects of the work and orders corrections. He is pleased with the villa and a surrounding colonnade and approves of the pavement. However, certain arched roofs (*camerae*) he finds unacceptable. After criticizing changes ordered by Quintus, Cicero further comments on Diphilus' work. He has failed to set up columns in the proper way, and they must be pulled down and replaced. Cicero attributes the faults to Diphilus' lack of skill with the plumb line (47). He concludes by saying that he hopes Diphilus' job (*opus Diphili*) will be done in a few months. The changes and repairs must have contributed considerably to the delay. Cicero notes that Caesius is supervising the job carefully (*curat*) and is reassured by this. Caesius is probably either an architect or a *uilicus* whom Quintus has left in charge of the job. Cicero never alludes specifically to Diphilus' actual method of employment, but the episode has many characteristics of *locatio* and perhaps he is a *redemptor* at work on contract (48).

(44) *Q.fr.* 2.6.3.

(45) On the plan, see *Q.fr.* 2.2.2. Longilius was probably the contractor for the major repairs. It is possible that contracts were also let for specialized finishing jobs. J. L. D. PEARSE, 22-23, thinks that Longilius was at least a *libertus* and possibly an *ingenuus.*

(46) *Q.fr.* 3.1.1-2.

(47) On final approval (*probatio*), see below at Chapter III, section C. Cicero seems quite confident in his ability to spot defects in the work. On the use of the *linea* by builders, see CATO, *Agr.* 14.

(48) J. L. D. PEARSE, 19-20, thought Diphilus an architect ; so too D. R. SHACKLETON BAILEY, *Cicero : Epistulae ad Quintum Fratrem et M. Brutum* (1980) 203. H. Loane (cited note 6), 86, calls Caesius an architect who "also served as *redemptor,* acting as go-between

In the same letter, Cicero mentions a different sort of construction problem and the two men in charge of it, Mescidius and Philoxenus ([49]). They have already built one watercourse on the Arcanum, a property in Arpinum, and Cicero consults them concerning the same type of job, this time on a nearby piece of property. The plan is to construct a duct to carry water from this estate to another, more arid one ([50]). Cicero discusses the job with Mescidius, who has measured the distance as approximately 3000 paces, and agrees to do the work for 3 sesterces a foot. Cicero has already summoned Cillo, another builder, who worked with a group of *conseruos et discipulos.* Unfortunately, four of his workers were hurt in an accident, and Cillo is unable to participate in the job. Exactly what his role would have been is hard to determine. He may have been a contractor who had done other work for Cicero ([51]).

Finally, in the same letter, Cicero describes a visit to Laterium where Quintus planned to build an *aedificatiuncula.* The *uilicus,* Nicephorus, had initially contracted to do the work for 16,000 sesterces ([52]). However, Cicero writes, Nicephorus subsequently withdrew from the contract because Quintus made additions to the work without any concomitant increase in price. It is almost certain that Nicephorus was a slave, but his status did not prevent him from undertaking a contract so long as he had a *peculium,* a special account granted by his master ([53]). Nicephorus saw this contract as a

for his master and the builder Diphilus". I think that this confuses the function of the architect as designer with that of the *redemptor,* who normally built under contract. The use of the term *curat* is familiar from inscriptions in which it designates the activity of the magistrate who supervises and approves the work (probably with the help of an architect). Caesius works in a supervisorial function (see also *Q.fr.* 3.1.2).

(49) *Q.fr.* 3.1.1. The status of these two men is impossible to determine, but J. L. D. Pearse, 23, speculates that Mescidius was *ingenuus* while Philoxenus was a slave or freedman. They do not seem to be members of the household.

(50) D. R. Shackleton Bailey (cited note 48), 204-205, discusses the name of the estate. Quintus wishes to establish a servitude on this property, see H. J. Roby, *CR* 1 (1887) 66-70.

(51) *Q.fr.* 3.1.3. S. Treggiari (cited note 25), 99, thought Cillo was a slave and a contractor ; so too M. L. Clark, *Architectural History* 6 (1963) 19. D. R. Shackleton Bailey (cited note 48), 205, raises the possibility that Cillo is freed and works with his former fellow-slaves (*conseruos*).

(52) *Q.fr.* 3.1.5 : *Tum is mihi respondit, se ipsum eius operis HS XVI conductorem fuisse, sed te postea multa addidisse ad opus, nihil ad pretium ; itaque id se omisisse.* On this passage, see further at Chapter III, section D.

(53) There is no unanimity about Nicephorus' status, but see R. Beare, *CQ* 28 (1978) 398-401, who concludes that *uilici* were always slaves ; H. Kaufmann, 210, thinks he was a slave with a *peculium* ; so too D. R. Shackleton Bailey (cited note 48), 206, and K. D. White, *Roman Farming* (1970) 350-354. S. Treggiari (cited note 25), 107, and J. L. D. Pearse, 25, both suppose that he was a freedman.

reasonably secure way to increase his *peculium.* However, he was knowledgeable enough to recognize that the changed terms of the contract were not in his interest. For Quintus, a contract with his *uilicus* was desirable because of proximity and familiarity. He clearly thought he could get more for less from Nicephorus. Quintus does not seem to contemplate using skilled slave labor for the job. Nicephorus himself would probably have had to hire *fabri* to help him do the job, and perhaps the cost of this caused him to rethink the advisability of the contract.

From this account we can see that Cicero commonly dealt with builders on hire. All of those he mentions by name are of indeterminate status, except for the slave Nicephorus, who alone can be linked to the household of either brother. In each instance, contractors, either as individuals or in a group, undertake jobs ranging in size and complexity from a watercourse to larger projects, such as Quintus' villa. Diphilus, although not specifically called *redemptor,* fits well the model of a building contractor : he is in charge of a whole project, he must pass an approval process and he is obviously a skilled worker, despite Cicero's criticisms. He could conceivably be working with assistants, but none are mentioned. Longilius, explicitly called *redemptor,* is at work on the house at Rome with many *structores.* The men who construct watercourses in Arpinum appear to work in groups, either as partners (Mescidius and Philoxenus) or as a workshop under the supervision of one person (Cillo).

It is not clear in each case what the actual expertise of the contractor is. The primary requirement would be knowledge of the basic skills required to erect walls upon foundations through the use of various common building materials such as stone or *opus caementicium.* Of course, the particular type of job conditioned the choice of a builder. Those such as Mescidius, Philoxenus and Cillo may have been especially experienced at building watercourses and tunnels. Longilius and Diphilus were probably trained in domestic and villa construction. In so far as the work consisted of *opus caementicium,* it is likely that it could progress with relatively few trained builders : one or two to direct the work, and others to help build the formwork and lay the courses of concrete ([54]). Stonework required a higher level of skill in building and more manual labour to transport the material.

(54) This process is depicted in the tomb of Trebius Iustus, see J. P. ADAM, *La Construction Romaine* (1984) 87. F. RAKOB in *Hellenismus in Mittelitalien* (1976), 366-378, has an important discussion of the changes in organization brought about by the use of *opus caementicium.*

In all of the above-mentioned cases, the units of production seem relatively small. Because of the labor-intensive nature of building, even when 'many builders' were at work on the houses on the Palatine (*Q.fr.* 2.5.4), the work was still not complete two years later. Private building was slow, and most employers would presumably rather not spend the money to bring in additional workers to speed the work ([55]). The contractors were also required to complete a certain amount of finishing, as Cicero implies in his comments about the work on Quintus' villa. Their contracts may have included specifications for this or provisions for the hire of specialized workers.

The organization of private building in the Empire is somewhat harder to reconstruct, particularly since there is no convenient literary account of the activities of any individual, as we find in the letters of Cicero. Aside from the *Digest* texts, the references to contractors and contracting are few and for the most part are from funerary monuments recording only the name and profession of the deceased. To a large extent it is impossible even to differentiate those who worked on private jobs from those who worked on public monuments. Therefore, I will consider all of the evidence, distinguishing the public from the private when possible.

Several references to *redemptores* indicate the types of projects for which they were engaged. One inscription from Narnia in the early third century A.D. mentions that Q. Parfidius Primus was employed as a *redemptor* for the construction of a villa. The inscription further records the presence of a supervisor : *agente Pauliniano* ([56]). At Capua, Lucceius Peculiaris, *redemptor proscaeni*, offered a dedication to the *genius theatri*. He was in charge of the construction of this part of the theatre, and his monument depicts the work in progress ([57]). An inscription from Cumae records the words *L. Cocc. ... redem(ptor)* ([58]). If this individual can be identified with L. Cocceius Auctus, a freed architect from Puteoli, he serves as an example of an architect who both designed structures and contracted for their construction ([59]). Strabo mentions a certain Cocceius who had built a tunnel between Lake Avernus

(55) A. Burford, *Craftsmen in Greek and Roman Society* (1972) 98-101, discusses the division of labour and the units of production which she thinks were generally small in both the Greek and Roman world.

(56) *CIL* XI 4127 = *ILS* 6027.

(57) *CIL* X 3821 = *ILS* 3662. The crane depicted on this monument is similar to the one on the monument of the Haterii, see J. P. Adam (cited note 54), 48-49.

(58) *CIL* X 3707.

(59) See *CIL* X 1614 = *ILS* 7731a. See Fabricius and Stein, *RE* s.v. Cocceius # 2 col. 129, and Groag, # 12 col. 129-130 (1901).

and Cumae in the age of Augustus. It is therefore conceivable that this person was a designer who specialized in tunnel construction ([60]).

A freedman, P. Cornelius P.l Philomusus, records that he worked as a *pictor scaenarius idem redemptor* on an inscription commemorating the construction of a monument for himself and his family ([61]). His particular area of expertise may have been as a painter, but he claims also to be a *redemptor* and therefore may have taken contracts both for construction and for painting. He could perhaps be identified with Philomusus in *CIL* VI 9851, a *redemptor* who erected something in honor of his patron and himself at Rome ([62]). C. Albius Torquatus referred to himself simply as *redemtor operis* (*sic*) in the second or third century. This is a standard title for a builder, but does not provide any further details about his employment ([63]).

Other *redemptores* are linked with public works through titles such as *redemptor operum publicorum*. Two freedmen, P. Turpilius A.l Phronim(us) and P. Turpilius A. l Niger, worked as *redemptores ab aerario*. Although they may have been hired by the *aerarium* to work on construction, the title does not indicate explicitly that they were builders ([64]). Three individuals are linked to public works and were hired either to do new construction or maintenance work. Q. Olius Princeps was a *redemptor oper(um) publicorum Lauiniorum*. Pearse dated the inscription to the early first century A.D. ([65]). P. Mucius Nedymus worked as a *redemptor operum Caesarum* at Reate ([66]). L. Paquedius Festus was a *redemptor operum Caesar(is) et puplicorum* (*sic*). His dedication to the Bona Dea is rather interesting because he seems to have participated in repair work on the *aqua Claudia*; this coincides with Frontinus' observation that the *curator aquarum* made use of *redemptores* ([67]). From Thuburbo Maius comes a bilingual inscription recording the

(60) STRABO 5.4.5. *CIL* X 6697 also records a L. Coc(ceius) involved in building in the reign of Hadrian.

(61) *CIL* VI 9794 = *ILS* 7672. J. L. D. PEARSE, 33, thought it unlikely that this individual was involved in construction. He probably supervised projects for decoration. So too I. CALABI-LIMENTANI (cited note 20), 67.

(62) *CIL* VI 9851.

(63) *CIL* IX 3650. There are other examples of *redemptores* which cannot be linked to construction : C. Hostius, a freeborn individual, calls himself a *redemptor* (*ILLRP* 773 = *ILS* 9040). *CIL* VI 9854 mentions M. Clodius Priscus, *redemptor a laco Fundano*. Two other inscriptions record the title of *redemptor, NS* 1923 pp. 19-20 and *CIL* VI 378.

(64) *CIL* VI 9852 a and b. F. MILLAR, *JRS* 54 (1964) 33-40, discusses the *aerarium* and its role in building.

(65) *CIL* XIV 2091.

(66) *CIL* IX 4694.

(67) *CIL* XIV 3530 = *ILS* 3512 = *I.It.* IV 1, 611. FRONTINUS, *Aq.* 119 ; 124.

hire of three natives for the erection of a *cella proma.* The Latin text parallels the usage commonly found in public contracts at Rome ([68]).

Only two inscriptions provide any interesting details about the family connections or employment of imperial *redemptores.* An imperial freedman, Ti. Claudius Aug. l. Onesimus, was both *redemptor operum Caesar(is)* and a magistrate of the *collegium fabrum tignariorum* at Rome in the eighteenth *lustrum* ([69]). He is the only example of a member of the *collegium* who can be linked with public contracting. The membership and activities of this *collegium* will be discussed at greater length below.

Q. Haterius Tychicus, a *redemptor,* has been identified as a member of the family of builders whose tomb depicts in relief sculptures a number of public monuments dated to the Flavian era ([70]). A scene on another part of the tomb portrays builders, doubtless members of the family, astride a large crane as if at work adjacent to the monument. The crane was used for lifting blocks of stone and is similar to that found on the monument of Lucceius Peculiaris (see above). It is now generally accepted that the relief sculptures represent projects on which members of the family worked, and that no other coherent topographical or thematic link exists between them. Coarelli has recently asserted that the family descended from the freedman of the *consul ordinarius* of 53, Q. Haterius Antoninus, who may have sponsored their contracting business and helped in obtaining state contracts ([71]).

There is very little to be deduced from these sources which adds to the model of private building we have seen in the letters of Cicero. The contractors seem to work in small units of one or two on whole projects. There is some evidence of specialization according to types of buildings and

(68) *AE* 1940, 16 = *ILTunisie* 732. J. L. D. PEARSE, 35, thinks this is not later than the first century A.D. In addition to the *redemptores* mentioned in the text, there are four *redemptores* who seem to have specialized tasks. Ti. Claudius Celadus was a *redemptor intestinarius,* see *AE* 1925, 87 = *NS* 1924 p. 348. This adjective seems to indicate that he was a joiner, *Cod. Th.* 13.4.2. Examples of *redemptores marmorarii* are : *CIL* VI 33873, Rome ; *CIL* X 1549, Puteoli ; *IRT* 275, Lepcis Magna.

(69) *CIL* VI 9034. It seems unlikely that he was, as R. MACMULLEN (cited note 5), 213, has said, a 'guildmaster', but the title *redemptor* shows how he made his living after manumission. Ti. Claudius Celadus (see above at note 68) may be another example of an imperial freedman who was also a *redemptor,* see H. LOANE (cited note 6), 83, and J. L. D. PEARSE, 34.

(70) *CIL* VI 607. On this identification, see F. COARELLI (cited note 20), 266-269.

(71) On the interpretation of the relief sculptures depicting monuments, see H. KAHLER, *MDAI* (1939) 264 n. 2 ; E. PARIBENI, *Atti IV Congr. Naz. Studi Romani* (1938) II 148 ; F. CASTAGNOLI, *BCAR* 69 (1941) 59-69 ; F. COARELLI (cited note 20), 266-267. On the implications of this identification for the building industry, M. STEINBY *ARID* Suppl. X-XI (1983) 219-221.

building materials. So, for example, L. Cocceius may have been an architect who also took contracts for construction, specializing in tunnel construction. Philomusus adds to the description of his skill as a painter the fact that he is a *redemptor*, indicating that he is a craftsman who is capable of organizing an entire job either of painting or building. Parfidius Primus was in charge of the construction of an entire villa. As *redemptor proscaeni*, Lucceius Peculiaris was either constructing one part of a new theatre or refurbishing an old *proscaenium*. The depiction of his workers and crane indicate that he was working largely in stone ([72]).

As for the status of these individuals, many are freedman and one or two are imperial freedmen. In general, freedmen are heavily represented among builders, perhaps predictably, in particular, during the first century A.D. As we will see below in the discussion of *fabri*, many of these people were trained as builders in the *familia* and upon manumission were able to establish themselves in contracting businesses with the help of their patrons for whom they would also continue to work occasionally.

While the information from the inscriptions adds little to our knowledge of private building, there are some important implications for the organization of public building involving the use of *redemptores* on hire. As we have seen, contracting was the most common way of organizing public works in the Republic. With the coming of the Empire, just when public building becomes so important in size and scale, few signs clearly point to typical patterns of organization. The emergence of an imperial bureaucracy must have altered many aspects of public building, but we cannot say with certainty how this affected the procurement of skilled builders. The need for contracting may have continued, as certain pieces of evidence suggest, but the scope of their use and their success in competing with other sources of labor are impossible to describe ([73]).

As the inscriptions show, several contractors claimed to work either for the *aerarium* or on public works. Among these are both independent contractors, such as the freed Turpilii and the Haterii, and at least one imperial freedman. In the case of the Haterii, the size and opulence of their monument, as well as the scope of the works on which they were employed, suggest that this must have been a relatively prosperous business. The most prominent edifice among those depicted on the tomb is the Colosseum. The sheer size of the project presented a staggering challenge to the capacity of

(72) There is a useful discussion of this type of crane in J. P. ADAM (cited note 54), 48-49.
(73) P. A. BRUNT (cited note 4), 84-88.

the state to organize materials and labor. As Cozzo has shown, this massive edifice was designed so as to be built in discrete sections which could be constructed simultaneously by autonomous teams of builders ([74]). The Haterii and other contractors filled the need for trained builders since it is unlikely that there was a sufficient number of skilled slaves and freed workers available and not employed by the *curatores* ([75]).

Clearly the significant new feature in the organization of public works in the Empire was the establishment of centrally organized maintenance boards under the supervision of *curatores.* This new system involved the state in a major organizational role which it had avoided under the republican contract system. Gangs of skilled slaves were essential to the maintenance and construction of public works in the Empire, and the treatise on the *cura aquarum* by Frontinus provides the only coherent description of how the system worked ([76]). There were two distinct *familiae* of slaves, about 700 in all, working under the *curator* and his staff. The first group had been bequeathed by Agrippa to Augustus and subsequently given to the state ; the second was established by Claudius. The slaves were trained in a variety of different jobs and spent a large amount of time simply maintaining the existing aqueducts which were subject to damage from many causes. Frontinus also mentions that *redemptores* were hired by the *curator* for the construction of aqueducts ; L. Paquedius Festus worked on the Aqua Claudia ([77]). It has been conjectured that contractors were used to construct the new aqueducts while the slaves were kept busy with maintenance ([78]). Evidently, other public works, such as road construction, continued to be let to contractors in the first century A.D., and we hear from Tacitus and Dio that Domitius Corbulo attacked the contractors (*mancipes*) and *curatores uiarum* for the bad condition of the roads ([79]).

(74) G. Cozzo, *Ingegneria Romana* (1928) 216-220. For a recapitulation of the discussion of the economic impact of the construction of the Colosseum, see J. Skydsgaard in *ARID* Suppl. x-xi (1983) 223-227.

(75) On slave *fabri,* see below at section III.

(76) J. L. D. Pearse, 40-41 ; T. Ashby, *The Aqueducts of Ancient Rome* (1935) 17-25, on the staff of the water board ; 34-47, on their construction activity.

(77) Front. *Aq.* 119 ; 124.

(78) O. Hirschfeld, *Die kaiserlichen Verwaltungsbeamten bis auf Diocletian*[2] (1905 ; repr. 1975) 273-284. T. Ashby (cited note 76), 41-42, assumes a large role for contractors in new construction.

(79) Tac. *Ann.* 3.31.5 ; Dio Cass. 59.15.4. On this Domitius Corbulo, *PIR*[2] D141 and R. Syme, *Tacitus* (1958) App. 83, 788. On road construction, *CIL* VI 8468/9 and 31338. In all cases the contractors are referred to as *mancipes.* Cf. the contract for the pavement of the Via Caecilia, *ILLRP* 465 = *ILS* 5799.

The evidence for imperial organization of building is restricted, but the office of public works headed by the *curator operum publicorum* had a role in organizing builders, laborers and supplies. Several texts from the *Digest* imply that the *curatores* dealt with *redemptores* and were in charge of paying them ([80]). The *curator* probably did not deal with the contractors personally, but relied upon his staff of *procuratores* and other subordinates who were more directly involved with the day-to-day problems associated with public works. While some of the skilled labor force came from slaves in the service of the *curator*, contractors seem to have been active in public works, particularly in new construction.

III. – Other Builders : *Fabri* and *Fabri Tignarii*

Among those who can be identified as builders, the most numerous are those referred to either as *faber*, a designation which could indicate any artisan trained to work with durable materials, or *faber* modified by the qualifying adjective *tignarius. Tectores* and *structores* are also trained builders or plasterers ([81]). These titles do not evoke typical patterns of employment, and the scope of their professional activity is broad, ranging from slave builder to contractor. When *fabri* appear in the context of building, they are usually mentioned generically, as a group, without much detail ([82]). They are always skilled workers and appear to undergo a period of training, probably in workshops under the tutelage of other builders or, if slaves, within the *familia* ([83]). The descriptions of their work are usually so brief that it is hard

(80) On the duties of *curatores* in regard to *redemptores*, Papirius Iustus, (2 *de const.*) D.50.8.11 (9) pr., and Ulpian, (3 *opinionum*) D.50.10.2.1, discuss their obligation to handle the financial dealings with contractors both in Rome and in the provinces. Pliny, *Ep.* 10.17b, mentions his concern with extracting more money from the *curatores operum* at Prusia by obtaining accurate measurement of buildings. On the *curator operum publicorum*, see A. E. Gordon, in *University of California Publications in Classical Archaeology* II, 5 (1952) 279-304. The inscriptions on *curatores* usually commemorate their selection of a site for a building. Practically nothing is known about the role of the staff in organizing building.

(81) On *fabri*, see P. Kornemann, *RE* s.v. *fabri* esp. col. 1888-1896 (1909) ; J. L. D. Pearse, 65-66, has tabulated all of the epigraphical references to builders. See also H. Loane (cited note 6), 79-85, and P. A. Brunt (cited note 4), 87-88. *Fabri* were skilled to work in stone or in *opus caementicium. Structores* could be builders (Cic. *Att.* 14.3.1 ; *Q.fr.* 2.5.3) or carvers and arrangers of food (Petr. 35.2). *Tectores* were generally plasterers (Var. *R.* 3.2.9 ; Vitr. 7.10.2 ; Ulpian, D.13.6.5.7).

(82) Cic. *Fam.* 9.15.5 ; Sen. *Ben.* 6.15.7-8 ; Vitr. 4.2.2 ; 9 *praef.* 6 ; Cic. *Att.* 4.3.2 ; *Phil.* 1.12.

(83) Cic. *Planc.* 62 ; Col. 11.1.5 ; Vitr. 2.1.6 ; D.17.1.26.8. There were variations in the degree of skill they possessed, Sen. *Nat.* 6.30.4.

to generalize about their hire. They can undertake work on *locatio conductio*, as Cato suggests ([84]). They also are hired on a daily basis as skilled labor by a main contractor. In his account of the maintenance of the temple of Castor and Pollux, Cicero mentions that the contract to straighten the columns of the temple involved the hire of some *fabri* for a few days work, and the language indicates that they were hired on a daily wage by the *redemptor* ([85]).

Fabri sometimes worked in association with architects, perhaps forming small businesses and providing both the design and building expertise ([86]). This arrangement is implied in a text from Aulus Gellius describing the beginnings of a building project. An architect and *fabri* are summoned to the house of Fronto, and they show him a number of plans for a bath he intends to build. He selects a plan and the architect gives him an estimate ([87]). The use of available plans was probably appealing to many landowners, particularly for such buildings as baths or *insulae* which tended to assume standard features. *Structores* and *tectores* appear in similar contexts, often with no details about their method of employment. They work along with architects, perhaps in small contracting companies. They are also found working with *redemptores*, either on hire or as slaves in a workshop ([88]).

The legal texts offer a little more information about the status and hire of *fabri*. They often seem to be slaves, working either for their master or loaned or hired to another for use. Builders themselves bought slaves whom they could train and put to work ([89]). Many *fabri* were freedmen and owed a certain amount of skilled labor to a patron if he were living. Some also pursued jobs independently of the patron although the extent of their autonomy depended upon the terms of manumission ([90]). As we can see, the

(84) CATO *Agr.* 14.3.

(85) CIC. 2 *Verr.* i.147 : *tantum operis in ista locatione fuit quantum paucae operae fabrorum mercedis tulerunt.*

(86) Col. 1 *praef.* 4 ; CIC. *Fam.* 9.2.5 ; GEL. 19.10.1-4 ; PL., *Mil.* 919.

(87) GEL. 19.10.1-4.

(88) On *tectores*, SEN. *Ep.* 90.8 ; CIC. *Planc.* 62 ; *structores* perhaps at work with the architect Corumbus, CIC. *Att.* 14.3.1 ; with a *redemptor*, CIC. *Q.fr.* 2.6.3.

(89) On the loan of a slave *tector*, see ULPIAN, (28 *ad ed.*) D.13.6.5.7 ; TREBATIUS, (cited by ULPIAN, 20 *ad Sab.*) D.33.7.12.5, and POMPONIUS, (33 *ad Sab.*) D.8.4.11.1, mention slave *fabri*. PAUL, (32 *ad ed.*) D.17.1.26.8, discusses the case of a *faber* who bought and trained a slave acting on mandate from a friend.

(90) JULIAN, (22 *dig.*) D.38.1.23 pr., and ULPIAN, (5 *disp.*) D.40.4.13.1, refer to the obligation of a *faber libertus* to provide his services to his patron. On this see P. A. BRUNT (see note 4), 89. J. H. D'ARMS, *Commerce and Social Standing in Ancient Rome* (1980), 140-148, provides a discussion of the differing views concerning the question of autonomy among freedmen. P. GARNSEY, *Klio* 63 (1981) 359-371, proposes that freedmen were not

term *faber* can refer both to free builders hired as day laborers and to slave workers. Some *fabri* were contractors, however, and one text refers to *fabri* at work on the contract of *stipulatio* ([91]).

The epigraphic evidence obtained from the monument of the Statilii Tauri provides a model for the training and use of *fabri* within a *familia* ([92]). This prominent family of the early Empire left in their monument in the Via Appia over four hundred inscriptions among which are the names of slave and freed builders. There are two slaves called *fabri tignarii*, three slaves called *faber*, a *faber tignarius* of indeterminate status and a freed *faber structor parietarius* ([93]). Freedmen of the family were also active in the *collegium fabrum tignariorum* and several of them are listed as members of the Roman *collegium* in the first century ([94]). The slaves were presumably either purchased as trained builders or trained within the *familia*. Those who were manumitted certainly continued to work in the business of the family, but may also have been able to pursue independent careers in construction, perhaps with the help of their patrons. The association of the freedmen of the Statilii with the *collegium fabrum tignariorum* indicates that they were somewhat prosperous.

The building interests of the family were sufficiently extensive to justify the maintenance of slave builders. T. Statilius Taurus (cos. II 26) was one of a group of supporters encouraged by Augustus to contribute to the beauty of the city by building. The family property included, among other things, *horti* on the Esquiline and the first stone amphitheatre in Rome ([95]). Family slaves

invariably obligated to their patrons to the exclusion of other opportunities ; see further in the work cited at note 38, 129-130.

(91) See JULIAN, (22 *dig.*) D.45.2.5. The parties stipulate for the builder's *operae*.

(92) On the family and their monument, see NAGL, *RE* s.v. Statilius (Taurus) col. 2196-2207 (1929) ; J. H. MORE (cited note 34), chapter 4. As PEARSE points out, 64-65, neither in this monument nor in others with a large sample of slaves are those associated with building particularly numerous, see the *fabri* in the *monumentum Marcellae, CIL* VI 4443 and 4446 ; *monumentum C. Annii Pollionis CIL* VI 7405 ; *monumentum Liuiae CIL* VI 3969.

(93) Slaves : *CIL* VI 6363-6365 ; 6283-6285 ; Freedmen : *CIL* VI 6354.

(94) Freed members of the Roman *collegium* : *CIL* VI 9405 = *ILS* 7238. See also T. Statilius L.l. Chrestus in C. PIETRANGELI, *BCAR* 67 (1939) 101-107, on a partial list of the *magistri* of the Roman *collegium* for the ninth *lustrum*. *CIL* VI 9412-9415 use the title *faber tignarius*.

(95) On the amphitheatre, built of stone in the Campus Martius, SUET. *Aug.* 29.5 ; *Cal.* 18 ; DIO 51.23 ; 62.18 ; TAC. *Ann.* 3.72 ; STRABO 5.3.8. The *horti* on the Esquiline are mentioned by TAC. *Ann.* 12.59 as a lure to Agrippina and a motivation for the prosecution of T. Statilius Taurus (cos. A.D. 44). A *forum Tauri* is known only from Medieval sources, G. B. DE ROSSI, G. GATTI, *BCAR* 18 (1890) 280-283. On the activities of the founder of the line, T. Statilius Taurus (cos. II 26), see R. SYME, *The Roman Revolution* (1939) 325 ; 380 ; 498.

also cared for the amphitheater which was destroyed in the fire of 64. It has been hypothesized that the Statilii Tauri also had interests in the importation of timber from Dyrrachium, and this connection with the trade in building materials doubtless increased their interest in construction. This was a lucrative type of trade and attracted more than one wealthy and well-connected family ([96]).

The only prominent group carrying any association with construction was the *collegium fabrum tignariorum.* The name *faber tignarius* means carpenter or builder who works with beams, but their area of expertise was not limited to carpentry. Gaius describes them as *omnes qui aedificarent* ([97]). There can be no doubt that here, if anywhere, we find a significant association of individuals connected to construction. However, interpreting the relationship between the *collegium* and the building industry presents certain difficulties since the actual function of the group is unclear and the relationship of the members to the building trade is neither secure nor easy to define. Were the members active builders, and, if so, what sort of projects did they work on ? Did membership in the *collegium* condition to any extent the type of building a member engaged in ?

It seems best to suppose, following Waltzing, that there was no connection between the collegial membership and the structure and the organization of construction ([98]). The membership did not furnish instruction in building or cohorts or corvées for building, and the *collegium* did not necessarily consist entirely of builders. There are a few examples of an individual belonging to more than one *collegium* so that the strict identification of the members as builders may not be accurate in every case ([99]). The function of the *collegium* was apparently social and was restricted to those who could make the contributions required of members. As Waltzing has pointed out, the social and cult activities of the *collegium* furnished the membership, which was largely made up of freedmen or freeborn individuals of low status, a source of recognition among fellow craftsmen. Although such people were prevent-

(96) On the possibility of connections with the timber trade in Dyrrachium, see J. H. D'Arms (cited note 90), 155-156.

(97) Gaius, (2 *ad legem 12 tabularum*) D.50.16.235.1 : *'Fabros tignarios' dicimus non eos dumtaxat, qui tigna dolarent, sed omnes qui aedificarent.*

(98) J. P. Waltzing, *Étude historique sur les corporations professionnelles chez les Romains* (1895-1900) I 181-195 ; II 119, discusses the functions of the *collegia,* disposing of most speculation that they were similar to guilds or societies devoted explicitly to furthering the goals of the trade. See also F. M. De Robertis, *Il fenomeno associativo nel mondo romano* (1955) 21 ff.

(99) R. Meiggs (cited note 17), 321-322.

ed from taking their place among the truly prominent because of their low status, membership in a *collegium* allowed the members to achieve a sense of belonging and recognition for success which could, in some cases, be measured in terms of substantial wealth ([100]).

The *collegium* at Rome, reorganized in 7 B.C., had a prosperous and numerous membership into the fourth century when the economic situation began to worsen, and various changes were made in the functions of the group ([101]). We are fairly well acquainted with the structure of the association, which Gaius, probably writing in the second century A.D., compares to a city (3 *ad ed. prou.*, D.3.1.4). At this time, the *collegium* had 1300 members, making it the largest of those known in Rome, divided into 60 *decuriae*, with 6 *magistri quinquennales* elected by the *ordo decurionis*, the 60 chiefs of the *decuriae*. Each *magister* had 6 patrons and a scribe. The college could own property and maintained a *schola* whose location is uncertain ([102]).

The membership of the *collegium* consisted of free born or freed individuals ([103]). In the first century A.D., several imperial freedmen are members. Only one, Ti. Claudius Onesimus, a *magister* of the college in the 18th *lustrum*, can be connected to building. As we have seen, he was also called *redemptor operum publicorum* and presumably undertook public contracts for construction ([104]). Two other members enhance the connection of the college with building. P. Cornelius Thallus, a *magister quinquennalis* in the 27th *lustrum*, seems to have come from a family of three generations of builders, as his funerary inscription suggests. Q. Haterius Euagogus, a *decurio* in the

(100) On the various payments made in order to enter and continue membership in a *collegium*, see WALTZING (cited note 98), I 450-454.

(101) The *collegium* at Rome was reorganized in 7 B.C., as now seems secure, S. PANCIERA (cited note 34), 271-280. In general on the *collegium*, see WALTZING (cited note 98), II 117-122 ; J. H. MORE (cited note 34) ; J. L. D. PEARSE (cited note 34), 100-123 and *BCAR* 85 (1976-1977) 163-176.

(102) J. P. WALTZING (cited note 98), II 117-119, discusses the structure of the college. The location of the *schola* is uncertain, but may have been near the Palatine or in the area around St. Omobono, see S. PANCIERA (cited note 34), 279-280.

(103) The membership included many freedmen as has long been recognized, H. GUMMERUS, *RE* s.v. *industrie* col. 1503 (1916) ; the earliest known freed *magister* may be from the second *lustrum* ; slaves seem not to have been members, see J. L. D. PEARSE (cited note 34), 112 ; 114-116.

(104) *CIL* VI 9034 and C. PIETRANGELI (cited note 94), 102-105, on Ti. Claudius Onesimus, see above p. 59. Other imperial freedmen are identified by Pietrangeli, on lines 62 and 67, Ti. Cl(audius) Aug. (lib.) in the seventeenth *lustrum* and T. Fl(avius) Aug. l(ib.) in the eighteenth *lustrum*.

first or second century, may have been attached to the family of builders active in the Flavian era ([105]).

The *collegium* at Ostia has left much more information concerning the status and activities of the *fabri tignarii.* Founded in the mid-first century A.D. (58-63), by the late second century the *collegium* numbered 350 members. In organization, the college was probably modeled on the Roman example and consisted of 16 *decuriae* of 22 each with 3 *magistri quinquennales* and *scribae.* There is some evidence that the college had patrons. The *collegium* experiences an abrupt decline in the third century owing to a general economic decline, exacerbated by the growing prominence of Portus as the center of activity on the mouth of the Tiber ([106]).

The wealth of the *collegium* is well known and is demonstrated by property holdings, dedications and the prosperity of individual members. The collegial *schola,* the Casa dei Triclini, was built upon a well-located piece of property bordering the forum ([107]). The dedications of the college to officials of the *annona* in particular indicate that they were looked upon with favor by the officials charged with maintaining the organization of grain movement in the city. The college also had *praefecti,* perhaps another sign of imperial interest or influence ([108]).

The membership at Ostia is similar to that at Rome in the high incidence of freedmen and provides graphic evidence of the possibilities for enrichment and social mobility among this group. Of the 32 known *magistri* of the college, those for whom status is indicated are freedmen, and eight presidents of the builders' association were also members of the Augustales, a group representing the pinnacle of honor accessible to freedmen ([109]). One *magister* at Ostia went on to become Augustalis at Aquae Sextiae ([110]). Two other *magistri* received the *ornamenta decurionatus,* an important honor "reserved

(105) On P. Cornelius Thallus, see above p. 51 and note 34. Q. Haterius Euagogus (*CIL* VI 9408) cannot be positively identified as a member of the family whose tomb is discussed above (page 59 and notes 70-71).

(106) On the Ostian *collegium,* R. MEIGGS (cited note 17), 319-321 ; F. WILSON (cited note 17), 41-68 ; J. L. D. PEARSE, chapter 5.

(107) On the Casa dei Triclini, see above at note 19.

(108) F. WILSON (cited note 17), 64 ; R. MEIGGS (cited note 17), 320.

(109) A. LICORDARI, *Rend. Accad. Naz. Lincei,* 8th series 29 (1974) 322-323 ; J. H. D'ARMS, *AJP* 97 (1976) 387-411. On the importance of membership in the Augustales as a significant indicator of prominence for freedmen, J. H. D'ARMS (cited note 90), 126-140, has an important analysis of the Ostian evidence. On this group, see R. DUTHOY, *Epigraphica* 36 (1974) 134-154.

(110) L. Antonius Epitynchanus, *CIL* XIV 296 = *ILS* 1916.

for wealthy and prominent freedmen, whose background in slavery prohibited them from holding local magistracies" ([111]). M. Licinius Privatus, one of these men, donated HS 50,000 to be *bisellarius in primis constitutus.* His sons and grandsons achieved the rank of *decurio* at Ostia while his grandsons entered the equestrian order. Another example of upward mobility among this group is P. Cornelius Architectianus, *decurio* and son of a *magister* ([112]).

While it is not surprising that those who call themselves builders achieved some prosperity in a town which had undergone rapid development for almost a hundred years, the role of the *fabri tignarii* in the organization of public or private building remains indefinable. If we can assume that the members of the college were builders, and this assumption may not be fully valid, the problem of how they functioned professionally is still unanswerable. Many were freedmen, who were trained as slaves presumably in order to work for their masters. The difficulty comes in understanding what manumission meant to them as professionals. Some continued to work within the family structure, which may have diminished their opportunities for autonomy and financial gain. But, as Garnsey has observed, little is known about the nature of the relationship between patron and freedman, and in particular about the status of the patrons and the degree of dependence or independence accorded the freedmen ([113]). So, in the case of the Statilii Tauri, there are a number of freed *fabri* from the household of a prominent family, but we do not know whether they set up their own workshops or devoted all their time to furnishing services to the family building enterprises. Other builders, such as those employed by Cicero, seem to be foreign, low in status or freed, but appear to work independently. The wealth of many of the *fabri tignarii* suggests that they worked autonomously in their own enterprises. All of the 350 members at Ostia were not as successful as M. Licinius Privatus, but many surely earned a reasonable living by building, working on projects ranging from small private structures to large public works ([114]).

In any case, can we say that any of these people worked as contractors ? This would depend on the degree of autonomy enjoyed by the builder and

(111) J. H. D'ARMS (cited note 90), 133. M. Licinius Privatus, *CIL* XIV 374 and 128, see D'ARMS (cited note 109), 411, on him and the other unnamed recipient.

(112) P. Cornelius Architectianus, *CIL* XIV 5. See above at p. 51 and note 34 on this family.

(113) P. GARNSEY (cited note 38), 129-130, makes this point in regard to freed businessmen, particularly those involved in the grain trade.

(114) P. GARNSEY (cited note 90), 359-371, suggests that prosperity is one sign of autonomy.

his ability to undertake projects as large as a house or *insula.* Beyond this, we would need to know a great deal more about individual cases of property exploitation at Ostia and Rome. Presumably some of the people who built *insulae* did so using their own slaves and freedmen. But, as we have seen, property owners may have found it convenient to hire contractors, and it seems likely that many *fabri tignarii* owed their prosperity to participation in building contracts in an environment of intense building when the demand for new housing must have created a ready market for skilled builders.

As indicated at the beginning of this chapter, no clear vision of the organization of the construction industry can be reconstructed from the evidence as it survives ; only a shadowy picture of predominant patterns of employment emerges. The state of the evidence is complicated by the inherent character of building which has, even in modern times, been one of the less easily or thoroughly rationalized industries. The demand for building is episodic, and builders are often hired for specific projects as the need arises and only for the duration of the job ([115]). Rarely have forces of skilled builders been continuously employed on private projects. This quixotic pattern of demand results in a rather idiosyncratic and atomised industry : units of production tend to be small, consisting of a few workers, perhaps under the supervision of a master builder or contractor. Most construction projects are organized on a small scale at the local level. For example, the city government of Epidauros gave a number of small contracts for different parts of the construction of the temple of Asklepios. Similarly, many large structures in Florence during the Renaissance were built by wallers hired on contract and supervising a small number of subordinates. In Victorian England, despite the emergence of master builders who kept large numbers of builders under continuous employment by speculating on suburban developments, the industry was largely populated with small-scale carpenters and joiners working with fewer than fifty builders ([116]).

The Roman construction trade probably also consisted largely of small enterprises, organized by individuals or in small groups or partnerships, the number of builders rising and falling according to the demand for building.

(115) On the relatively slow rationalization of this industry, R. GOLDTHWAITE (cited note 1), 115-124 ; cf. the composition of the building industry since World War II, P. J. CASSIMATIS (cited note 1), 1-29.

(116) A. BURFORD (cited note 1), chapters 4-7 ; R. GOLDTHWAITE (cited note 1), 124-156 ; on the situation in Victorian England, H. DYOS (cited note 1), 641-690, especially at 652 : "Clearly enough, the most impressive feature of the industry as revealed in this way was not that the few were so large but that the many were so small". On the development of the 'master builder', E. W. COONEY (cited note 1, 1955-56), 167-176.

The composition of this 'building trade' would have been mixed, consisting of slave, freed and free builders, with a wide variety of organizational capability. Contracting is most fully attested in all sources as an important organizational mode since it can be detected not only in epigraphic and literary sources but also in legal texts. As we have seen, contracting could be used to organize the construction of jobs varying widely in size and complexity, from projects like watercourses to entire *insulae* or villas. The typical size of a workshop is impossible to estimate, but in general contractors appear to be skilled workers themselves, employing subordinates and perhaps supervising other builders on contract for specialized skills. Many of the contractors known to us are freed slaves, who may have themselves created workshops with their own slaves. Their level of prosperity would depend upon the size of the jobs they could undertake.

For those builders like the *fabri* and *fabri tignarii* who are not identifiable as contractors, it is practically impossible to discern any typical pattern of employment. Some were clearly contractors, whether through *locatio* or *stipulatio.* Free builders who were not contractors probably worked for a daily wage on small jobs or repair work or found employment with contractors. There is no evidence to suggest that any of the prominent *fabri tignarii* organized projects larger than an individual building, for example, as speculative developers of an entire neighbourhood. The more lucrative opportunities were presumably found in public building, which had the capacity to generate long-term employment. Some projects, as, for example, the Colosseum, appear to have been organized in sections which could be worked by individual contractors.

Other builders worked as slaves or free workers under a master builder or in a household. Slaves played a large part in building either as members of an upper class family with building interests or in a household of builders. The range of slave employment was wide ; many probably worked individually within their own skill on family projects. In the Empire, certain essential services generated the need for more rationally organized construction crews. The establishment of the *familia* of slave builders and technicians who were to maintain the aqueducts is the only well-documented example of this. This system was not always adequate for the size of the job, however, and from time to time, additional workers had to be hired to keep the aqueducts in shape and to build new ones.

While much of Roman private building was probably carried out by individual builders or small-scale entrepreneurs, it seems certain that the size and composition of the industry did not remain static over the period of the late Republic and early Empire. In fact, the building trade appears to have profited from a long boom in both public and private construction ([117]). The demand for private construction came from various sources : fires, floods and earthquakes necessitated rebuilding and repair ; an increasing population required housing. To fill these needs, some shoddy, rapidly built habitations shot up. Vitruvius, for example, complains of the use of wattle-work walls (*parietes craticii*) as a cheap and fast building technique ([118]). This sector of the building industry may have been highly speculative, and various attempts to regulate the quality of construction seem not to have been uniformly successful ([119]). New construction was also generated by many public monuments and works, both in Rome and nearby, such as the creation of the port at Ostia.

The development of *opus caementicium* allowed Roman builders and architects to provide salutary and attractive solution to the problems posed by the growth of the urban populace. The turning point came during the reign of Nero after the fire of 64, as concrete *insulae* began to become common at Rome ; the excavations at Ostia and the evidence of increasing production of brick for facing material attest to an active period of building. *Opus caementicium* was less labor-intensive than the more durable and expensive materials like stone, while safer and more practical than the cheaper techniques. It also required few skilled workers ([120]). This technique, along with

(117) M. Steinby, in *ARID* Suppl. x-xi (1983) 219, hypothesizes a boom in construction during the late first and early second centuries A.D., based upon the large production of bricks ; see also H. Bloch, *I bolli laterizi e la storia edilizia romana* (1947) 334-337, and T. Helen, *The Organization of Roman Brick Production* (1975) 18-20.

(118) Vitr. 2.8.20. On fires, floods and other natural disasters, see L. Homo, *Rome impériale et l'Urbanisme dans l'Antiquité* (1951, repr. 1971) 269-282. On shoddy construction practices and crowded urban conditions, see P. A. Brunt in *Studies in Ancient Society* (ed. M. I. Finley, 1974) 74-102. A. G. McKay, *Houses, Villas and Palaces in the Roman World* (1975) 80-99, and Z. Yavetz, *Latomus* 17 (1958) 500-517, give many sources for the bad living conditions prevalent in late republican and early imperial Rome, see Juv. 3.193-256 ; Pliny *Nat.* 36.106 ; 36.176.

(119) The production of housing may have been highly speculative, see T. Helen (cited note 117), 16-20. On attempts to regulate height and other building practices, see L. Homo (cited note 118), 533-566 ; the most notable instances were the legislation of Augustus limiting the height of structures to 70 feet, Suet. *Aug.* 89 and Strabo 5.37 ; the legislation of Nero after the fire of 64, Tac. *Ann.* 15.43-46 ; Trajan restricted buildings to 60 feet, Tac. *Hist.* 3.71 ; *Epit. de Caesaribus* 13.13 ; Pliny *Nat.* 35.173. On the situation at Ostia, G. Hermansen (cited note 18), 91-96.

(120) The use of *opus incertum* and *opus reticulatum*, which Vitruvius discusses (2.8.1), had become widespread by his time, see M. Torelli, in *Tecnologia, economia e società nel mondo romano* (1980) 139-159 ; F. Rakob (cited note 54), 366-378, on the consequences of this new technique for builders. On the new face of the city, see Tac. *Ann.* 15.43 and W. L. MacDonald, *The Architecture of the Roman Empire*[2] (1982) 25-31.

the development of relatively standarized forms of *insulae*, must have lent an element of predictability and quality to the process of building, particularly in comparison to other methods of construction.

This upsurge in building presumably altered the configuration of the construction trade to a remarkable degree. Entry into the building industry was probably relatively simple, and this factor, combined with the increasing amount of work available during the high Empire, made construction an attractive source of livelihood. The membership of the *collegium fabrum tignariorum* is probably the most significant surviving indication of the condition of builders during this period. With their relative prosperity, their association as members of a skilled work force and their large membership relative to other *collegia*, this group suggests the emergence of an active building trade with at least a rudimentary sense of professional identity.

CHAPTER III

Legal Problems Arising from Construction Contracts

SECTION A
TERM AND DELAY

One of the most significant sources of litigation in construction arises from the builder's failure to complete his work to schedule and the employer's concomitant attempts to mitigate the possibility of financial loss as a result of the builder's delay. Some employers could accept delay as a mere inconvenience, as did Cicero when he reported to Quintus that the builder at work on his brother's villa was outdoing himself in slowness : *In Maniliano offendi Diphilum Diphilo tardiorem* (*Q.fr.* 3.1.1-2). But the legal sources suggest that employers were not inclined to be indulgent of delaying builders. If an individual had relied upon the builder's promise to complete the work by a certain date and made arrangements for habitation or commercial use of the building, the contractor's delay could be costly. Of course, the builder had his own worries. His work could only be carried out during half of the year, and he could be hindered by the weather, the supply of materials and the availability of workers and machines (1). Events could often conspire to prevent the timely completion of the work, and the builder would have to face the consequences of a suit for defaulting on his obligation.

The jurists handle the problems of timely completion most frequently in regard to *stipulatio* although the issue also arises in *locatio conductio.* The emphasis upon ascertaining delay in *stipulatio* is prominent because the builder's performance is evaluated chiefly in terms of his ability to complete the work on time. The following discussion will focus first on the general practice of setting the term and the normal procedure when default occurs. Then we will consider a particular area of interest for the jurists : how to determine when a suit could be initiated on a contract lacking a completion date. The texts dealing with this problem indicate that some controversy

(1) According to FRONTINUS, *Aq.* 123, the building season for aqueducts was from April first to November first owing to the curing time required for *opus caementicium.*

arose among the jurists as they sought to mediate between the demands of timely completion and the need for safe, careful construction. Finally, we will examine cases involving the contractor's delay in stipulations for propping up *insulae* in imminent danger of collapse.

I. – Setting the Term

Construction contracts usually contained a clause setting a date for the completion of the job. Contracts for public works during the Republic give two examples of such clauses, which include a date and the words *dies operis* (2). In public law, the magistrate in charge of letting the contract fixed the contract term. This practice is illustrated in Cicero's description of Verres' notorious supervision of the contract for the upkeep of the Temple of Castor and Pollux during his urban praetorship of 74 B.C. (3). Verres wished to discourage contractors from bidding on a contract to repair the temple so that he could award the job to Habonius. (Habonius had already agreed to divide the contract price with Verres.) Verres achieved this result by setting a very brief term for the work, approximately two and a half months, thereby deterring any other contractor from assuming a contract with so short a term (148). Habonius took the contract, and no further mention was made of the term until, Cicero relates, the work was finally approved four years later. The demand for approval came from Habonius, who threatened Verres with exposure of their collusion (149). This is an instructive example both of magisterial rigour and discretion in the administration of public works.

In private law, the contract term was probably fixed in a more flexible manner, particularly since the parties had in principle to agree upon this term. In *locatio*, the *dies operis* was named in a *lex locationis* (D.19.2.13.10 ; D.19.2.24 pr.). If a contract contained this clause, the jurists did not allow the employer to sue in anticipation of the worker's default ; he had to wait until the full contract period had elapsed (D.19.2.13.10). Alternatively, the employer could extend the time limit if he chose to do so (implied in D.19.2.24 pr.). The contract could also be supplemented with stipulations specifying various penalties to be paid in the event of the builder's default (D.45.1.72.1 ; 45.1.113 pr.). But the employer could bring no suit either on

(2) The *lex parieti faciundo Puteolana* : *FIRA* III # 153 = *ILLRP* 518. The contract for the maintenance of the Temple of Castor : Cic. 2 *Verr.* i 148.

(3) Cic. 2 *Verr.* i 130-150. References to specific passages in this account are included in the text in parentheses.

the principal obligation or on the ancillary stipulations before the completion date had passed ([4]).

Stipulations for construction also commonly specified a completion date (D.5.1.43). As in *locatio*, the full contract period had to elapse before the stipulator could sue for default, as a text from Papinian demonstrates.

> Papinian, (2 *def.*) D.45.1.124.
>
> *'Insulam intra biennium illo loco aedificari spondes ?' ante finem biennii stipulatio non committitur, quamuis reus promittendi non aedificauerit et tantum residui temporis sit, quo aedificium extrui non possit : neque enim stipulationis status, cuius dies certus in exordio fuit, ex post facto mutatur. idque et in 'stipulatione iudicio sistendi causa facta' placuit, scilicet ut ante diem stipulatio non committatur, si certum esse coeperit parere stipulationi residuo tempore non posse.*

The latter portion of the text has been suspected of interpolation, but this is not relevant to our discussion ([5]). The builder has promised to construct an *insula* within a period of two years. According to Papinian, even if no construction work has been done, and the remaining time left in the contract is not sufficient to allow construction of the *insula*, the stipulator cannot sue before the contract period is complete.

This is a clear example of strict interpretation of the words of the promise. The jurist is not willing to alter the terms of the agreement by allowing the employer to bring an early action in anticipation of the ultimate failure of the builder to finish the work. In order to sue, collect damages and presumably continue building with another contractor, the employer must wait the full two years. While this could be a disadvantage, the obvious security of a completion date gave the parties a fixed limit to look to and allowed them to avoid uncertainty concerning the exact term of the obligation ([6]).

II. – Determining Delay in the Absence of a Fixed *Dies operis*

Both in *locatio conductio* and in *stipulatio* it was possible to form a valid contract without including a fixed completion date. The parties sacrificed a certain security in doing this, but they also left more room for flexibility as

(4) On the calculation of damages and penalties for delay and on D.19.2.13.10, see below at Chapter III, section E.

(5) R. Knütel, *SP* 91-92, and C. A. Cannata, *Colpa* 157-159.

(6) R. Knütel, *SP* 92, points out the underlying importance of D.45.1.41.1 (cited below at note 13) for this text ; the stipulator had framed the agreement and therefore no extension of the date should be granted at his request.

the contract period progressed. For example, in D.45.1.124, the stipulator was committed to a builder for two years ; he might have avoided his later dilemma by not setting a completion date. The employer also had the option of adding a *dies operis* to the contract by appending a subsequent *pactum*, provided that the builder agreed upon this (7).

Ideally, the absence of a time limit need have had no material effect if the builder made progress in fulfilling his obligation within a space of time acceptable to the employer. If, however, the employer sensed that little or no progress was being made, he might be anxious to bring an action against the builder for default. The lack of a clear completion date forced the employer to consult the jurists about when to sue, since an action would center upon deciding whether or not the builder had defaulted.

One source on construction in *locatio conductio* refers to a contract which lacks a specific completion date :

> Labeo, (4 *post. a Iau. epit.*) D.19.2.58.1
>
> *In operis locatione non erat dictum, ante quam diem effici deberet : deinde, si ita factum non esset, quanti locatoris interfuisset, tantam pecuniam conductor promiserat. eatenus eam obligationem contrahi puto, quatenus uir bonus de spatio temporis aestimasset, quia id actum apparet esse, ut eo spatio absolueretur, sine quo fieri non possit.*

The text is sound (8). The parties have concluded a contract for a job through *locatio conductio* without specifying a completion date. Subsequently, they have made a *stipulatio* for *id quod interest* payable to the employer if the work is not completed (9). The employer evidently wishes to win his interest

(7) On the modification of the agreement through the addition of a subsequent *pactum*, see F. DE ZULUETA, *The Roman Law of Sale* (1945) 53-54, and M. KASER, RPR^2 I 487 and 527, with bibliography.

(8) G. BESELER, *TR* 10 (1930) 183, preferred to omit the reference to the *uir bonus*, a phrase which he considered a Justinianic interpolation ; so too E. ALBERTARIO, *Studi di diritto romano* III (1936) 285-310. F. HORAK, *Rationes decidendi* I (1969) 220-221, thinks the text may have been reworked. Many scholars have argued for its genuineness : T. MAYER-MALY, *LC* 111-112 ; C. A. CANNATA, *Colpa* 169 ; R. KNÜTEL, *SP* 132 n. 49. F. M. DE ROBERTIS, *I rapporti*, 69 ; 110-111, implies his acceptance of the substance of the text.

(9) On the commonplace use of ancillary stipulations to ensure a fixed payment to the *locator* in case of the builder's delay, see below. R. KNÜTEL, *SP* 132-133, has argued recently that the stipulation in D.19.2.58.1 was to guarantee interest money if the work did not conform to the specifications of the contract. But it seems to me that the language of the text and the similarity of the stipulation to others commonly in use in construction to guarantee the employer against delay argue against his interpretation. The employer already had the contractual remedy of *probatio* built into the agreement in case of faulty or non-conforming work. For a fuller discussion, see below at Chapter III, section E.

damages by claiming that the builder has defaulted. The jurist is being asked to decide whether or not the stipulation has fallen due.

The text may retain the opinion of Labeo, although it is also possible to suppose that Javolenus is responding to a more restrictive opinion of the earlier jurist ([10]). The jurist suggests that in determining the question of default the contract term should correspond to the length of time a 'good man' would consider suitable. This implies a two-step procedure in deciding an employer's action : first the length of time suitable for the performance should be estimated, then the builder's work must be measured against this standard. If the builder had exceeded a reasonable time limit, he would be responsible for the employer's interest.

The jurist justifies the use of this standard by inferring from the content of the stipulation *id quod actum est*, 'what was done' ([11]). He assumes that the parties had intended to allow the builder an adequate amount of time to complete the project. This interpretation relies upon their good faith and builds into the stipulation the idea that a reasonable time should be allowed the builder to complete his work. The use of good faith in interpreting stipulations is less common than a strict enforcement of the agreement. He defends filling the gap in this way on the grounds that he is preserving the intent of the parties. As we will see, the recourse to a 'good man' standard was coming increasingly into use as a technique for estimating the contract term in stipulations for construction. In D.19.2.58.1, the stipulation is appended to a good faith contract, a fact which probably affected the interpretation of the stipulation.

While the text itself offers no reason for the omission of a specific *dies operis*, several explanations for this are possible. At the time of the formation of the contract, the employer may have had no particular interest in the completion of the work by a certain date. The subsequent addition of the stipulation for *id quod interest* suggests that he became concerned about the consequences of delay in the work and wished to supplement the remedy available through the *actio locati*. Alternatively, the omission may reflect

(10) The fragment comes from Javolenus' epitome of Labeo, and there is some question as to which jurist is the author of the response. The fragments of Javolenus' epitome of the *Posteriores* divide themselves into two groups ; D.19.2.58 belongs to the group bearing the inscription "Labeo libro *post. a Iau. epit.*". These texts may contain Labeo's comments introduced by verbs in the first person. On the difficulty of distinguishing the responses of the two jurists, see F. SCHULTZ, *History* 207 ; P. JÖRS, *RE* s.v. Antistius # 34 col. 2548-2557 (1894) ; A. PERNICE, *Labeo* I 69-70. T. MAYER-MALY, *LC* 111, attributes the opinion to Labeo.

(11) On *id quod actum est*, see F. PRINGSHEIM, *SZ* 78 (1961) 83-85.

disagreement between the parties about the length of the term. If, for example, the contractor was agreeable to all other contract terms but this one, the employer may have preferred to leave the question of a completion date unsettled in the hope that no problem would arise from this gap. Disagreement forced the parties to seek from the law a resolution of the ambiguity in the contract. This solution may have been preferable to an enforced wait of two years before any action could be brought for delay.

For *stipulationes* lacking a completion date, the general rule was that the *stipulator* could bring an action immediately ([12]). But it was recognized that the variable content of stipulations often made immediate fulfillment physically impossible, and different rules were developed for obligations whose execution required the performance of an inherently time-consuming activity. A typical hypothetical circumstance of this type is an obligation made at Rome to pay a sum (*dare*) at Ephesus or some other distant locale. In these situations, the jurists allowed a *diei adiectio*, a postponement of the fulfillment date, because of the element of time implicit in the obligation ([13]).

Stipulations for construction were recognized as promises whose execution implied a term of some length, and by the high classical period the jurists had adopted the technique of filling in the completion date when it was lacking :

> Paul, (24 *ad ed.*) D.45.1.73 pr.
>
> *Interdum pura stipulatio ex re ipsa dilationem capit, ueluti si id quod in utero sit aut fructus futuros aut domum aedificari stipulatus sit : tunc enim incipit actio, cum ea per rerum naturam praestari potest. sic qui Carthagini dari stipulatur, cum Romae sit, tacite tempus complecti uidetur, quo perueniri Carthaginem potest. item si operas a liberto quis stipulatus sit, non ante dies earum cedit, quam indictae fuerint nec sint praestitae.*
>
> Pomponius, (5 *ad Sab.*) D.45.1.14
>
> *Si ita stipulatus essem abs te 'domum aedificari ?' uel heredem meum damnauero insulam aedificare, Celso placet non ante agi posse ex ea causa, quam tempus praeterisset, quo insula aedificari posset : nec fideiussores dati ante diem tenebuntur.*

(12) Pomponius, (5 *ad Sab.*) D.50.17.14 : *In omnibus obligationibus, in quibus dies non ponitur, praesenti die debetur.* See M. Kaser, *RPR*[2] I 638 n. 35.

(13) Ulpian, (50 *ad Sab.*) D.45.1.41.1 :

> *Quotiens autem in obligationibus dies non ponitur, praesenti die pecunia debetur, nisi si locus adiectus spatium temporis inducat quo illo possit perueniri. uerum dies adiectus efficit, ne praesenti die pecunia debeatur : ex quo apparet diei adiectionem pro reo esse, non pro stipulatore.*

See M. Kaser, *RPR*[2] I 239.

The first text is sound ([14]). Paul observes that a *pura stipulatio*, one not limited by a fixed date or condition, often takes a certain interval of time for completion. Appropriate examples are promises for things that do not yet exist : anything *in utero*, future fruits, or a house not yet built. The stipulator has an action only when that period of time has elapsed which is implicit in the nature and content of each obligation ([15]). Although this is rather vaguely formulated, it does seem to preclude the possibility of an action early in the contract when delay is merely incipient.

In the second text, Pomponius cites Celsus on the appropriate moment for an action in two similar factual circumstances. In the first hypothetical case, a builder has promised on *stipulatio* to build a house ; in the second, an heir has been instructed to build an *insula*. The formulation is so brief that we can only assume that in each case the obligation to build carries with it no fixed term for completion. Celsus prefers to allow the action only when the sufficient time has passed for the construction of an *insula*. The fact that Celsus is cited in an epitome of Sabinus' works and the way in which he is introduced into the text (*Celso placet*) indicate that there may have been a difference of opinion between the jurists upon this point. Perhaps Sabinus allowed an earlier suit when delay became apparent. His view may have been excised in preference to Celsus' opinion which became the prevailing classical view ([16]).

This text has been considered interpolated, and a recent challenge to the authenticity of the text has been raised by Cannata. He finds troublesome the apparent incongruity in the two hypothetical situations forming the basis of the case. Cannata would rewrite the text expunging the stipulation for construction as an inappropriate and inaccurate analogy, particularly because the rest of the text and Pomponius' fifth book *ad Sabinum* pertain to testamentary law ([17]).

(14) T. Mommsen read *potuerit* for *potest*. C. A. CANNATA, *Colpa* 159 n. 2, deletes *tunc enim-potest* as a gloss, objecting particularly to the use of the expression *per rerum naturam*. However, this phrase seems acceptable, if somewhat vague, when used in reference to the characteristics of the *pura stipulatio* (see CELSUS, D.50.17.186, cited next note), and *PS* 3.4b.1 ; 4.11.8.

(15) CELSUS, (12 *dig.*) D.50.17.186 : *nihil peti potest ante id tempus, quo rerum naturam persolui possit : et cum soluendi tempus obligationi additur, nisi eo praeterito peti non potest.*

(16) Sabinus may have discussed the interpretation of *dies* and *diei adiectio* in stipulation, as the commentaries by Pomponius and Ulpian reveal, see above notes 12 and 13 and O. LENEL, *Paling.* II 96 and 1195.

(17) C. A. CANNATA, *Colpa* 159-163, discounts this text as a pertinent source based upon his conviction that the classical jurists preferred to allow an action before the sufficient time had passed. He therefore considers interpolated any reference to a stipulation for construction. On Cannata's technique, see the useful comments of R. KNÜTEL, *SP* 133 n. 51. There is

It is, however, possible to defend the soundness of the text on the grounds that the situations are procedurally similar. The first case involves a stipulation for the construction of a house, and the problem is familiar enough by now : when can an action begin on a stipulation lacking a completion date ? In the second case, a testator imposes upon his heir the duty to build an *insula* for a third party through *legatum per damnationem.* In this case, the legatee is seeking an action against the heir for failure to produce the *insula.*

The action for *legatum per damnationem* was the *actio ex testamento,* in this case for an *incertum.* Scholars have long observed the similarities between this action and the *actio ex stipulatu* ([18]). There is evidence that the jurists frequently recognized these similarities and extended the law in one area through analogy to the other ([19]). The difficulties of delay, so common in stipulation and *locatio conductio,* would be no less problematic for the legatee in this case. Both actions had a *formula incerta* and involved damages for delay ([20]). If the wording of the obligation contained no completion date, the legatee would need a way to determine when to bring suit against the heir, and the solution similar to that applied in stipulation may have appeared suitable.

Celsus establishes that the builder cannot be sued for delay until the sufficient time has passed for completion of the building, and then introduces into the discussion a further consideration. Most builders were required to procure sureties who would secure the builder's ability to pay damages if he did not fulfill his obligation. They were equally responsible with the builder for these damages. Celsus prevents the stipulator from suing sureties before the adequate time had elapsed ([21]).

All of these texts refer to the 'adequate' or 'natural' period of time implied by the physical requirements of construction, but no method or standard for

something awkward about the text, see T. MAYER-MALY, *LC* 99, who, along with H. SIBER, *Römisches Recht* II (1928, repr. 1968) 253 n. 4, expunges *uel-aedificare* ; R. RÖHLE, *SD* 34 (1965) 204 n. 88, defends it along lines similar to those proposed here. The fact that Celsus refers only to the *insula* (omitting the *domus*) indicates that he was responding to the case of the heir. Pomponius extended the opinion by the inclusion of the first *si*-clause in order to reflect the dominant classical view on the question of an early suit against a delaying builder.

(18) O. LENEL, *EP* 367-368 ; L. MITTEIS, *SZ* 32 (1911) 1-23 ; M. KASER, *RPR*[2] I 743.

(19) L. MITTEIS (cited note 18), 1-11, uses the example of how the term *dies cedit* came into stipulation from the law of succession but lost the technical meaning it had when used in contrast to *dies uenit.*

(20) See M. KASER, *SZ* 67 (1950) 346-347, on damages for delay in *formulae incertae.*

(21) On the obligations of sureties, see below at Chapter III, section E.

estimating the necessary time emerges. In D.19.2.58.1, Labeo, or Javolenus, resorted to the *arbitrium boni uiri* as a standard for gauging the contract period, a technique which relies upon the good faith nature of the contract. The employer cannot expect to bring an action as soon as he perceives delay, but must wait a reasonable time before he can establish default.

The jurist Venuleius recommends a similar technique for use in determining the 'natural' time required for the fulfillment of an obligation in stipulation. In a series of texts extracted from his first book *On stipulations*, Venuleius begins with an example of a contract for the payment of a fixed sum at a distant locale and then proceeds to contracts for construction.

> Venuleius, (1 *stip.*) D.45.1.137.2
>
> *Cum ita stipulatus sum 'Ephesi dari ?' inest tempus : quod autem accipi debeat, quaeritur. et magis est, ut totam eam rem ad iudicem, id est ad uirum bonum remittamus, qui aestimet, quanto tempore diligens pater familias conficere possit, quod facturum se promiserit, ut qui Ephesi daturum se spoponderit, neque duplomate diebus ac noctibus et omni tempestate contempta iter continuare cogatur neque tam delicate progredi debeat, ut reprehensione dignus appareat, sed habita ratione temporis aetatis sexus ualetudinis, cum id agat, ut mature perueniat, id est eodem tempore, quo plerique eiusdem condicionis homines solent peruenire. eoque transacto, quamuis Romae remanserit nec possit Ephesi pecuniam dare, nihilo minus ei recte condicetur, uel quia per ipsum steterit, quo minus Ephesi daret, uel quoniam per alium Ephesi possit dari uel quia ubique potest soluere : nam et quod in diem debetur, ante solui potest, licet peti non potest. quod si duplomate usus aut felici nauigatione maturius quam quisque peruenerit Ephesum, confestim obligatus est, quia in eo, quod tempore atque facto finitum est, nullus est coniecturae locus.*

The text is concerned primarily with establishing the method for estimating a time limit on a case-by-case basis ([22]). Venuleius uses the standard hypothetical case of a stipulation for the payment of a fixed sum at Ephesus : how much time should be allowed for the completion of the obligation ? Venuleius advises that the entire matter be left to the *iudex* to decide ; he is to evaluate the case in the manner of a *bonus uir*, a good man, by judging the promissor's behavior according to the example of what a *diligens pater familias* would have done in the same position. This investigation involves

(22) C. A. CANNATA, *Colpa* 109-112 and *SD* 32 (1966) 99-102, recapitulates most of the textual criticism of this text. See also the *Index Interpolationum* with a complete list of proposed interpolations. Among the major criticisms are the following : G. BESELER, *SZ* 51 (1931) 196 and *Das Edictum de eo quod certo loco* (1907) 96-97 ; V. ARANGIO-RUIZ, *Bull.* 25 (1912) 152 and *Resp.* 184-189.

taking into account the particular facts of individual circumstances in order to ascertain whether the promissor had accomplished his goal *eodem tempore, quo plerique eiusdem condicionis homines solent peruenire.* The success of the stipulator's case depends upon the judge's estimation of the timeliness of the promissor's performance.

Many objections have been raised to the soundness of this text ([23]). In particular, the references to the *uir bonus* and the *diligens pater familias* have been noted as possible interpolations. But as D.19.2.58.1 and numerous other texts show, the good man's judgment was often used as a standard for judging behavior in contractual relations. The classicity of this usage is now accepted ([24]).

Venuleius introduces into the text the *diligens pater familias* as a model of reasonable behavior by which the promissor's performance could be judged. The *iudex* must estimate how much time a 'diligent' person would have required to travel to Ephesus and discharge his debt. He must determine the facts of the case as best he can and compare the promissor's behavior to that of an ordinary but diligent individual. The *iudex* may take into account such factors as the weather and season as well as the health and physical condition of the promissor. The text gives no indication of the basis for the promise to pay money at Ephesus, but it seems likely that some sort of commercial transaction generally gave rise to stipulations of this sort. A ready model for the judge was furnished by the normal practice in seaborne transport and trade, which often involved obligations to be discharged at remote locations. Information such as the length of a typical voyage under varying circumstances was available from shippers or other people who customarily made these trips. Some of this business was doubtless discharged by procurators, slaves or freedmen acting in behalf of a principal. An allusion later in the text to the possibility that the principal may have someone make the payment for him hints at this practice ([25]).

(23) W. KUNKEL, *SZ* 45 (1925) 305-308, and S. SOLAZZI, *L'Estinzione dell' obbligazione nel diritto romano*[2] (1935) I 98-101, are both disturbed by the use of 'abstract standards' in the text. Kunkel discards references to the *diligens pater familias* as representative of post-classical attempts to introduce a *diligentia*-standard into the law. Solazzi finds D.45.1.137.2 in complete contradiction to other texts on the problem of term, especially D.45.1.41.1 and 13.4.2.6. C. A. CANNATA, *Colpa* 109-112, also considers most of the text interpolated.

(24) On the use of the *arbitrium boni uiri,* P. VOCI, *Le obbligazioni romane* I.1 (1969) 190-229 ; F. GALLO, in *Studi G. Grosso* III (1970) 477-542. See further on the use of this technique in construction contracts below at Chapter III, section C.

(25) On seaborne commerce in general, see J. H. D'ARMS and E. C. KOPFF edd., *The Seaborne Commerce of Ancient Rome : Studies in Archaeology and History* (1980). On the use

Venuleius' opinion was obviously just one possible solution to the problem of estimating when a suit on this type of obligation should take place. The use of the phrase *magis est* indicates that there was controversy, and the emphatic and detailed nature of Venuleius' response may result from his eagerness to assert his point of view. Other jurists were probably willing to grant an early action, especially if the promissor had made no attempt to fulfill his obligation ([26]). In these cases, the stipulator doubtless exerted pressure so as to obtain an action when the delay became evident. In addition, there may have been reluctance on the part of the jurists to introduce into the law of stipulation such an important and emphatic use of a good faith technique, essentially forcing the stipulator to assume the promissor's good faith in awaiting the performance of the obligation. Venuleius is trying to inject an element of trust and reliance into contractual obligations concluded through stipulation. But many individuals probably preferred to contract through *stipulatio* precisely because of the strict nature of the obligation and they would be reluctant to accept an interpretation of the contract which allowed the promissor a 'reasonable time' even if his delay was apparent.

Against the background of this text, the next case in this line is particularly important :

> Venuleius, (1 *stip.*) D.45.1.137.3
>
> *Item qui insulam fieri spopondit, non utique conquisitis undique fabris et plurimis operis adhibitis festinare debet nec rursus utroque aut altero contentus esse, sed modus adhibendus est secundum rationem diligentis aedificatoris et temporum locorumque. item si non inchoetur opus, id tantum aestimetur, quod in illo interuallo effici potuit. transactoque tempore quo insulam consummare oportuerit, si postea aedificetur, liberetur reus, sicut liberatur, qui se daturum spopondit, si quandoque tradit.*

Venuleius turns to an obligation for the construction of an *insula* ([27]). The first half of the text (through *temporum locorumque*) echoes the earlier

of slaves or freedmen as intermediaries in commerce, see J. H. D'Arms, *Commerce and Social Standing in Ancient Rome* (1981) ; cf. P. Garnsey in *Trade in the Ancient Economy* (edd. P. Garnsey, K. Hopkins, C. R. Whittaker, 1983) 118-130.

(26) There seems to have been some resistance to the idea that there could be no suit before the sufficient time for the performance had elapsed, see Ulpian, citing Julian, (27 *ad ed.*) D.13.4.2.6. See below at section III.

(27) This text has been much criticized. G. Beseler, *SZ* 45 (1925) 439 ; H. Siber (cited note 17), 253 n. 4 ; W. Kunkel (cited note 23), 307 ; V. Arangio Ruiz, *Resp.* 182-184. All object primarily to the phrase *diligens aedificator.* So too C. A. Cannata, *Colpa* 152-154, who thinks the locution *secundum rationem diligentis aedificatoris et temporum locorumque* illogi-

section in D.45.1.137.2 in which the jurist outlines the points to be examined in estimating the length of time a *diligens pater familias* would need to get to Ephesus. In this instance, he describes the procedure for estimating the appropriate time for completing a construction project. The builder should not be encouraged to hasten his progress by every available method, for example, by hiring extra *fabri* or day laborers. He must instead behave in the manner of a *diligens aedificator* and in accordance with the exigencies of locale and weather.

The use of the *diligens aedificator* provides a *iudex* with a way of mediating between a very strict interpretation of the contractor's duty and an interpretation which takes into account the factual background of the case. This is typical of the jurists' handling of many problems associated with building. The use of an 'ideal type' allows the judge flexibility in gauging the builder's progress because he is using as a standard behavior which corresponds to that normally expected from a good builder in similar circumstances ([28]). This is not an exceedingly high level of conduct, but one which incorporates an element of good faith in assessing the builder's behavior. Venuleius clearly was familiar with the problems associated with construction and knew something about the organization of construction projects. He is deliberately attempting to incorporate usages of the trade into the judge's evaluation of the builder's progress and is also concerned with promoting good construction practice. As a result of Venuleius' opinion, employers would hesitate to bring an early action and would be inclined to wait until some-

cal, and the *diligens aedificator* a superfluous abstraction rather than a meaningful addition. The phrase may not be elegantly composed, but seems to yield the meaning, "according to the manner of a diligent builder and taking account of the times (comprising the season and weather) and of the location". On this, see R. KNÜTEL, *SP* 133 n. 51, who presumes that the text is sound.

(28) The use of types like the *bonus uir* and the *diligens aedificator* characterizes the law-making of the Roman jurists as that of 'ordinary observers' rather than as 'scientific policymakers'. On the utility of this distinction in understanding Roman jurisprudence, see B. W. FRIER, *LTIR* 46-47 ; on this distinction in general, see B. ACKERMAN, *Private Property and the Constitution* (1977) 10-22 : The ordinary observer tends to establish "principals that best characterize the structure of socially based expectations" using language which makes sense in terms of ordinary discourse in society (p. 14). The idea that artisans should be held to a standard of quality which is generally held to be adequate is stated by ULPIAN, (1 *ad ed. aed.*) D.21.1.19.4 :

> *Illud sciendum est : si quis artificem promiserit uel dixerit, non utique perfectum eum praestare debet, sed ad aliquem modum peritum, ut neque consummatae scientiae accipias, neque rursum indoctum esse in artificium : sufficiet igitur talem esse, quales uulgo artifices dicuntur.*

thing like a 'reasonable time' had passed. Builders would gain a certain amount of protection from the need to work under the pressure of an imminent action.

In the latter portion of the text, Venuleius deals with the discharge of the contract and the purging of delay, as does another text from Paul (cited below). If the stipulator initiates an action before the reasonable time required for the physical act of construction, and no work has yet been done, Venuleius would only allow an estimation of the value of what could have been constructed in the elapsed time. This is what the phrase *item – effici potuit* seems to mean. Thus, in a limited context, Venuleius appears to allow an action before the 'reasonable time', but would deny full completion costs to the stipulator.

As the final sentence of D.45.1.137.3 indicates, if the reasonable time had elapsed, the stipulator was not forced to bring an action, and the builder could still fulfill his contract by completing the structure, so long as the obligation had not been extinguished by an action. Paul gives a decision similar to that in Venuleius' text :

> Paul, (74 *ad ed.*) D.45.1.84
>
> *Si insulam fieri stipulatus sim et transierit tempus, quo potueris facere, quamdiu litem contestatus non sim, posse te facientem liberari placet : quod si iam litem contestatus sim, nihil tibi prodesse, si aedifices.*

This text has not been severely criticized ([29]). Paul says that the builder may continue to discharge his obligation by building so long as the stipulator has not completed proceedings *in iure* and received a formula for the trial (*litis contestatio*). After this point, the builder cannot hope to complete the job. The *litis contestatio* marks the point at which the builder's obligation is extinguished. Thereafter, he will, if condemned, be required to pay a judgment.

The rules emerging from these texts can be summarized as follows :

1. If a stipulation contained an express completion date, the jurists did not allow an action before the full term had run (D.45.1.124). If two parties have made a stipulation for a construction project, but the promise contains no date of completion, the inherently time-consuming character of the obligation requires a *diei adiectio* to set a time limit (D.45.1.41.1). In these cases, the prevailing view is that the stipulator can only initiate his *actio ex*

(29) R. KNÜTEL, *SP* 187-188, and C. A. CANNATA, *Colpa* 154.

stipulatu if such time has elapsed as would be sufficient for the builder to finish the job (D.45.1.73 pr. ; 45.1.14 ; 45.1.84). But there are hints of controversy, and in some cases an early suit might have succeeded particularly if no work had yet been done (implied in D.45.1.14 and D.45.1.137.3). There is some indication that the builder would only be responsible for a *pro rata* portion of the building costs.

2. In the course of the action, the *iudex* was instructed to make an estimation of the 'natural' time required for the completion of the contract. One method of calculating the appropriate contract term was to exercise the judgment of a 'good man' and evaluate the builder's performance against the standard of what a normally functioning builder would have accomplished under similar conditions (D.45.137.2-3). The use of this standard was first found in stipulations for penalties appended to construction contracts in *locatio conductio* (D.19.2.58.1). Venuleius encouraged the use of the *arbitrium boni uiri* in judging stipulations. There may have been some resistance to the use of this technique.

3. Once delay was apparent, the employer could still choose to ignore it and allow the builder to continue building and to secure a release from liability (D.45.1.84 ; 45.1.137.3). The contractor could keep trying to complete his work and purge his obligation unless the stipulator initiated an action. At the conclusion of *litis contestatio*, the contractor did not have the right to continue his work, and any work done subsequent to this time would not be counted in an estimation of his damages.

III. – Limiting Cases : Delay in Propping Up Collapsing *Insvlae*

Despite the relative consensus in the surviving juristic sources on the need to allow an adequate period of time before bringing an action, the opinions in D.45.1.14 and D.45.1.137.3 imply that there were challenges to this position. This resistance to postponing suits where delay is apparent emerges in cases dealing with contracts to prop up collapsing apartment blocks. In these situations, the jurists were willing to limit the amount of time allowed to the builder for the completion of his job :

Marcellus, (20 *dig.*) D.45.1.98.1

> *Ex hac stipulatione : 'insulam fulciri spondes ?' quando nascatur actio, quaeritur. et utique non est exspectandum, ut ruat : nec enim nihil stipulatoris interest fultam potius esse, quam non esse : nec tamen recte agetur, si nondum praeterierit temporis tantum, quo fulcire potuerit redemptor.*

Ulpian, (20 *ad ed.*) D.45.1.72.2

> *Plane si 'insulam fulciri' quis stipulatus sit, non est exspectandum, ut insula ruat, sic deinde agi possit : nec 'insulam fieri', ut tantum temporis praetereat, quanto insula fabricari possit : sed ubi iam coepit mora faciendae insulae fieri, tunc agetur diesque obligationi cedit.*

In the first text, which has never been considered interpolated, and in the first part of D.45.1.72.2, the cases are identical. Both concern stipulations for propping up an *insula*, and neither obligation appears to include a fixed term. The jurists determine when the *actio ex stipulatu* can begin ([30]).

Marcellus points out that the stipulator should not await the collapse of the building before initiating the action. He maintains, however, that the builder is to be allowed an adequate period of time for the completion of his work. In this opinion, he alludes to the rules already established in regard to construction.

It is clear from the text, however, that Marcellus is aware of the different concerns underlying a contract for propping up a building. The *insula* is in danger of imminent collapse, and Marcellus emphasizes the stipulator's strong interest in avoiding the large financial loss which could result from the destruction of an *insula.* The rule in this case enforces the implicit 'reasonable' time required for the work, but the owner is also encouraged to be watchful and to take steps quickly if the builder delays.

In the second text, Ulpian's treatment of the same factual circumstances preserves the admonition that an action not be delayed *ut insula ruat* ([31]). The text omits Ulpian's conclusion about when an action can begin, and this opinion must be inferred from his response to the second factual situation in the latter portion of the text. In the case of the stipulation to build an *insula,* Ulpian goes on to state explicitly that the stipulator need not be compelled to postpone commencement of the action until an adequate time for reconstruction has passed. The obligation falls due (*dies cedit*) when a

(30) The text is sound, see C. A. CANNATA, *Colpa* 155.

(31) S. SOLAZZI (cited note 23), 98 n. 2, considers this text contradictory to the rest of classical thought on the subject and therefore marks *nec insulam – cedit* as an interpolation. C. A. CANNATA, *Colpa* 155-159, takes a different view, seeing Ulpian's opinion here as representative of the classical doctrine ; he therefore considers contradictory, and interpolated, all the other texts discussed above (for example, D.45.1.73 pr. ; 45.1.14). It seems far more likely that the prevailing view in the *Digest* sources is the one I have described here, namely that early suits are discouraged until a 'reasonable time' has passed. The discontinuity evident in the texts signals juristic controversy, and the actual state of juristic thought on the question was doubtless more complex and disputed than the sources indicate.

mora faciendae insulae begins to be apparent. The same rule certainly applies to the first case as well.

Ulpian's rule stands in sharp contrast to the trend of thought which appears to dominate the texts in the *Digest.* His point of departure in the text is fundamental in shaping the outcome of the case. He wants to shorten the time horizons of the obligation by concentrating upon the employer's potential loss. A collapsing *insula* is the extreme example of a situation in which the builder's delay would be extremely costly. Ulpian extends his case to consider stipulations for construction as well and allows the employer to sue as soon as the builder's delay becomes evident. The employer would have to calculate his interest in extinguishing the obligation by an action : this recourse may have been worthwhile if the employer was in a hurry.

There was evidently a considerable difference of opinion among the jurists concerning the proper handling of these cases. On the one hand, certain jurists strove to guarantee the builder a reasonable time. Many of these opinions assumed a situation in which the builder has been at work but is pressured by the employer. They emphasize careful construction practice and the preservation of the agreement and prefer not to interfere in the execution of it. On the other hand, Ulpian represents another set of concerns. He maintains that an action is appropriate the moment delay becomes apparent. The employer's interest in quick execution of the agreement is paramount. Evidently, factual situations and specific cases would influence the outcome of a suit of this sort since there was not a solid consensus on this point, and the builder and employer would each have had to take chances on the wisdom of omitting a fixed completion date.

SECTION B

THE LIABILITIES OF THE PARTIES DURING THE CONTRACT TERM

Many of the legal disputes represented in the juristic sources on construction contracts originate at the end of the contract term when the employer evaluates the builder's work to determine its state of completion and conformity with the agreement. These disputes arise, for example, if a contract clause has been interpreted differently by each party, or if the quality of the work does not seem to meet the employer's expectations.

Another source of legal difficulty in construction stems from the nature of the building process itself as a slow and risky business, susceptible to a variety of assaults by nature. Often the completion of a project is hindered or rendered impossible by events which are not necessarily attributable to the behavior of either party. In these cases, extra expense is always the result, and each party faces the threat of a potential financial loss or decrease in his original expectations. The employer, hoping to obtain the object he had commissioned at the original price, will attempt to hold the builder to the agreement. The builder seeks to earn his full pay without having to suffer any loss for extra repairs or completion costs.

In the actual judicial process, the task of the *iudex* in these situations is rather difficult. He does not need to resolve questions of fact, such as how well the building conforms to the plan. He must resort to a broader principle for determining who bears financial loss when neither party is necessarily at fault. The jurists devote a number of texts to the responsibility for damage sustained by the structure during the contract term. In these opinions, a significant evolution is perceptible in classical jurisprudence which reflects changing patterns of liability in construction contracts in *locatio.* The jurists begin from a relatively undifferentiated conception of the builder's responsibility as encompassing risk for the totality of the project. The earliest stage, represented by Labeo, appears to accord the builder a broad liability for all aspects of the contract : the employer can expect that the builder will be totally responsible for the completion of the job. Gradually, inroads are made into this responsibility by the introduction of mitigating factors designed to limit the builder's overall liability ([1]).

(1) Most scholarly discussion of the texts presented below has aimed specifically at deriving a uniform classical rule on the question of the parties' liability for *periculum.* The most

The first juristic opinion on the builder's risk for his work comes from Labeo, who responds to an inquiry concerning a watercourse which has been destroyed by a landslide.

Labeo, (1 *pith.*) D.19.2.62

Si riuum, quem faciendum conduxeras et feceras, antequam eum probares, labes corrumpit, tuum periculum est. PAVLVS : immo si soli uitio id accidit, locatoris erit periculum, si operis uitio accidit, tuum erit detrimentum.

I will discuss only the opinion of Labeo in the first half of the fragment ; the second half of the text is considered below. The first part has not been suspected of interpolation ([2]). A builder has completed the watercourse for which he had contracted, but he has not yet had it approved. A landslide (*labes*) has either destroyed the conduit or seriously undermined it. Labeo assigns the *periculum* for this to the contractor ([3]).

Because the cause of the *labes* is rather mysterious, the meaning of Labeo's decision has been the subject of various interpretations. Most scholars have agreed with Kaser that *labes* is equivalent to *uis maior*, a sort of act of God. If *labes* is interpreted in this way, Labeo stands alone among the jurists in assigning this responsibility to the builder ([4]). Cannata and Wubbe have rejected this interpretation although they differ slightly in their analysis of the cause of the landslide. Cannata attributes the *labes* to faulty workmanship ; Wubbe interprets it an accident, which may have arisen because of faulty

comprehensive treatment is in M. KASER, *SZ* 74 (1957) 155-200, especially 186-194, on *locatio conductio operis.*

(2) There is a consensus on this, see M. KASER (cited note 1), 186-194, and, most recently, M. PIETSCH, *Die Abnahme im Werkvertragsrecht* (diss. Hamburg, 1976) 25.

(3) *Periculum* designates the burden of risk alloted to the party who must bear the costs of damage to the work, see HEUMANN-SECKEL, s.v. *periculum*: "tragen des durch Zufall entstehenden Schadens". However, *periculum* may not be restricted to the context of accidental damage ; it seems to denote the risk for any damaging circumstance occurring before the final approval. Modern scholarship has attempted to find a comprehensive technical meaning for *periculum* ; this has been an unfruitful search owing to the sheer number and diversity of contexts in which the term is used. See G. MACCORMACK, *SZ* 96 (1979) 129-172, a study of *periculum* in contract law, and, *Bull.* 21 (1979) 11-37, in other areas of law.

(4) M. KASER (cited note 1), 188-190. Many recent discussions rely upon Kaser's interpretation either explicitly or implicitly, see M. PIETSCH (cited note 2), 25-26 ; J. A. C. THOMAS, 682 ; R. RÖHLE, *SD* 34 (1965) 206 and 214-216 ; E. BETTI, *SZ* 82 (1965) 13-18 ; I. MOLNÁR, *ANRW* II 14 (1982) 651-660 ; J. MIQUEL, *SZ* 81 (1964) 184-187, comes to similar conclusions about the text citing V. ARANGIO RUIZ, *Resp.* 189. See also on this text, S. MARTIN, *Law and History Review* 4 (1986) 419-433.

construction (5). Both are correct in asserting that the details of the text mitigate against interpreting the landslide as a result of *uis maior.* However, the facts of the case fail to indicate clearly that the builder was at fault. In the following analysis, I follow another possible line of reasoning.

Two aspects of the text are especially worthy of attention. First, the word *labes* is extremely vague and cannot, in the absence of any other information, be automatically interpreted as an instance of *uis maior.* The word itself can encompass several types of phenomena ranging from an earthquake to a defect in the soil caused by a natural weakness or by erosion. Furthermore, the use of *uis maior* as an exculpatory circumstance seems not to have been introduced into discussions of *locatio conductio operis.* There is no reason to suppose that Labeo, who was familiar with this category from other areas of law, intended to allude to *uis maior* simply by this reference to a landslide (6).

Secondly, the type of construction is important. The inclusion of the detail that the contract was for the construction of a *riuus* indicates that the case was taken from or based upon a real factual situation (7). The facts of the case are few, but they nevertheless leave open the possibility that the construction of the watercourse caused the landslide. The specific problems posed by watercourses were well known, and Vitruvius emphasized that they required particularly solid construction (8). If the construction were on sandy soil, instead of cut from rock, the fabric would be of concrete faced with some type of material and lined with *opus signinum.* To avoid slippage, the conduit would have to be water-resistant and set along a gentle grade. Roman engineers were aware of the increased weight of these conduits when filled

(5) C. A. CANNATA, *Colpa* 219-222 ; F. B. J. WUBBE in *L'Homme dans son Environnement/Mensch und Umwelt* (1980), 134-135, says Labeo was thinking about 'eine *Panne*' and was not concentrating on either faults of nature or of man ; elsewhere, however, he attributes the destruction of the *riuus* to technical failings ("wegen einer technischen Unzulänglichkeit") p. 138.

(6) M. KASER (cited note 1), 189, recognized this ambiguity as do many now, see, for example, I. MOLNÁR (cited note 4), 651-652 ; F. B. J. WUBBE (cited note 5), 134-135. *Labes* could occur either as the result of an earthquake or spontaneously and was often interpreted as a portent. See further below on D.19.2.33 (cited note 21) in which *labes* is used to indicate *uis maior.*

(7) Generally, the word *opus* is used ; other references to specific types of structures include *domus* and *insula,* see above at Chapter I. The classification of the *Pithana* as a work is debated. P. JÖRS, *RE* s.v. Antistius # 34 col. 2551-2552 (1894), thought the work contained cases taken from everyday life for use as a manual ; F. SCHULZ, *History* 226-227, considered the work 'casuistic'. A. PERNICE, *Labeo* I 35-36, thought it theoretical in nature.

(8) VITR. 8.6 especially section 1 ; see L. CALLEBAT, *Vitruve de l'Architecture, Livre 8* (1973). On the construction of aqueducts, see T. ASHBY, *The Aqueducts of Ancient Rome* (1935) 42-44, and E. VAN DEMAN, *The Building of the Roman Aqueducts* (1934) 3-21.

with water, and took pains (not always successfully) to avoid building up pressure within the channel. Labeo makes it clear that the landslide follows the completion of the work immediately. The most obvious conclusion to draw from this situation is that the soil was too unstable to bear the weight put upon it : an internal weakness in the building site was made manifest by the construction of the watercourse. This is an extremely common problem in construction even today when more sophisticated soil and geological analysis is possible ([9]).

If this analysis of the situation underlying the text is correct, Labeo holds the builder responsible for damage caused by a weakness in the building site. To put this in more general terms, Labeo construes the builder's liability for the job quite broadly. He doesn't explicitly examine factors which might mitigate the builder's responsibility, such as the presence or absence of fault, or the forseeability of the accident ; he prefers to assign risk based upon a notion of the builder's sphere of control. He may have reasoned as follows : the contractor had control of the land (furnished by the employer) and of the work (because of the contract) ; any damage arising while the job was under his control was his responsibility because he accepted the work *ut artifex*, as a skilled professional. Perhaps Labeo thought that the builder should have anticipated the accident, particularly given the enhanced risks involved in the construction of watercourses ([10]). In any case, this text establishes the builder's basic liability for the work and the building site and confirms the employer's desire to leave everything in the contractor's hands. As we will see, this view is altered over the course of time.

The jurists began to limit the liability of the builder before *probatio* when certain types of events prevented the fulfillment of the contract :

(9) See M. S. SIMON, *Construction Contracts and Claims* (1979) 135-150, on changed conditions ; I. VERNON WERBIN, *Legal Phases of Construction Contracts* (1961) 38-45, on increased cost of work owing to unforeseen conditions. Borings or other tests are commonly made to ascertain the stability of the site. The builder is often held liable for his failure to foresee problems, particularly if his inspection of the site was not adequate. He may escape liability in certain circumstances, for example, if he has been furnished inaccurate information about the building site by the employer.

(10) On the assignment of liability based upon a concept of risk rather than according to causal factors, see T. HONORÉ and H. L. A. HART, *Causation in the Law*[2] (1985) 308-324, and P. ATIYAH, *An Introduction to the Law of Contract*[3] (1981) 212 : "... a person who undertakes to do something takes the risk that performance of his undertaking may prove more onerous than expected, or even impossible, as a result of changes in circumstances which are normal, or merely slight deviations from the normal". Labeo may have considered the landslide within the normally expectable consequences of the contract.

Javolenus, (5 *Lab. post.*) D.19.2.59

Marcius domum faciendam a Flacco conduxerat : deinde operis parte effecta terrae motu concussum erat aedificium. Massurius Sabinus, si ui naturali, ueluti terrae motu hoc acciderit, Flacci esse periculum.

Marcius contracts with Flaccus for the construction of a house. When the work is partially complete, the structure is destroyed by an earthquake. Javolenus cites the opinion of Sabinus, who attributes to Flaccus, the employer, the *periculum* for the damage caused by *uis naturalis.*

The text has obviously been abbreviated as the syntax of the final phrase indicates. Massurius Sabinus is the subject of the sentence, but his opinion, expressed in the indirect statement (*Flacci esse periculum*), has no governing verb. Since Javolenus cites Sabinus in an epitome of Labeo's *Posteriores*, an earlier, unabbreviated version probably contained an opinion of Labeo followed by that of Sabinus introduced by a verb such as *respondit.* Subsequently, the compilers or early epitomators removed Labeo's opinion from the text ([11]).

The factual situation differs in two respects from that in D.19.2.62. First, the structure, a house rather than a watercourse, is only partially built. Second, the cause of the damage is an earthquake and not a landslide. The first difference does not appear to influence the jurist's decision. The reference to the partial state of completion simply serves to indicate that the damage occurred before *probatio.*

Consideration of the second difference, earthquake instead of landslide, leads to the heart of the distinction emerging in this and subsequent texts. The factual situation is less ambiguous than in Labeo's case : an earthquake cannot have been caused by construction, while a landslide might have been. Sabinus takes this specific example and creates an exception to the builder's generalized liability for damage, introducing *uis naturalis* as a category of events outside the contractor's sphere of control.

If an earlier version of this case did contain an opinion of Labeo, are we to assume that there was some controversy between the two early classical

(11) M. Kaser (cited note 1), 191, accepts the authenticity of the substance of the text and argues that an opinion of Labeo has been excised. Most subsequent scholarship has accepted this view, see C. Alzon, *Labeo* 12 (1966) 330 ; R. Röhle (cited note 4), 214, agrees with Kaser and reads <*si operis uitio, Marci*> at the end in anticipation of Paul's note on D.19.2.62. See also S. Martin (cited note 4), 430-431. C. A. Cannata, *Colpa* 225-226, who disagrees with Kaser concerning D.19.2.62, goes on to deny that Labeo could have proposed the antithesis to Sabinus' opinion, asserting that such an opinion never existed and would be uncharacteristic of Labeo ; cf. J. A. C. Thomas, 682.

jurists regarding *uis naturalis*? Kaser has argued that Javolenus excised as outmoded an opinion similar to that in D.19.2.62, in which Labeo attributes to the builder liability for *uis maior.* Since, according to the argument advanced earlier in this chapter, it was not Labeo's intent to discuss *uis maior* specifically in D.19.2.62, we might also want to reconsider on what grounds Sabinus may have differed with Labeo ([12]).

Perhaps Sabinus intended to distinguish between different factual situations which led to different conclusions of law. By this analysis, Sabinus recognized the difference between *labes*, an ambiguous event perhaps linked to the construction, and *uis naturalis*, a disaster of natural origin. Some critics of this text have objected to the phrase *ueluti terrae motu* as a gloss ([13]). But Sabinus was simply repeating from the hypothesis the specific situation in order to elucidate further his distinction between the situation in Labeo's text and the new category of *uis naturalis.* He does not define or expand this category to include other types of destructive events (for example, storms or fire) or criteria of foreseeability and resistability, as Servius did in D.19.2.15.2 ([14]). In all of the cases pertaining to construction, the range of exculpatory *uis* seems to remain closely associated with problems connected with the building site. The new category of *uis* was quickly accepted and applied by subsequent jurisprudence.

A qualification of Sabinus' decision is preserved in Javolenus' commentary on Cassius' *Ius Ciuile*:

> Javolenus, (8 *ex Cassio*) D.19.2.37
>
> *Si, priusquam locatori opus probaretur, ui aliqua consumptum est, detrimentum ad locatorem ita pertinet, si tale opus fuit, ut probari deberet.*

The factual situation is similar to those in the previous texts : the building is damaged or destroyed before *probatio* by 'some force' (*uis aliqua*). The jurist

(12) See M. Kaser (cited note 1), 191 ; F. B. J. Wubbe (cited note 5), 139-141, offers a different interpretation. He thinks that Labeo would have always attributed to the employer the risk for loss caused by an earthquake (to be differentiated from the situation in D.19.2.62). Sabinus (and Javolenus) agreed, but narrowed the category of landslide to include only those caused by *uis naturalis.* There is, of course, no evidence that Labeo ever considered the problem of *uis maior* arising from the building site in relationship to contracts for construction. On Labeo's treatment of *uis* in other circumstances, see D. Nörr, *Festschrift für Franz Wieacker zum 70 Geburtstag* (1978) 115-144.

(13) See M. Kaser (cited note 1), 191, who refutes this view with further bibliography. The expression *uis naturalis* occurs nowhere else in the *Digest.*

(14) The bibliography on D.19.2.15.2 is extensive, see M. Kaser (cited note 1), 169-175, and most recently P. W. de Neeve, *SZ* 100 (1983) 296-339, with good bibliography. See T. Honoré and H. L. A. Hart (cited note 10), 245-290, on risk and forseeability.

says that the employer must bear *periculum* if the work was such that it ought to have been approved. The text has been criticized, but Kaser maintains that the sense is genuine although there are traces of post-classical abbreviation ([15]). Nothing compels us to doubt the classicity of the substance of the decision. Röhle attributes the interpretation in the text to Cassius, and this may be correct although it is impossible to distinguish between the decisions of Javolenus and Cassius ([16]).

Despite the apparent similarities to D.19.2.62 and 19.2.59, the vagueness of this text makes it somewhat harder to interpret. The details present in the earlier cases are lacking : no specific type of structure is mentioned ; the degree of completion is unstated ; the agent of destruction is simply *uis aliqua.* The case may have been invented by Cassius as a hypothetical limiting case to Sabinus' opinion in D.19.2.59.

The jurist attributes to the employer the loss (*detrimentum*) under one condition : the work must be such that it ought to be approved ([17]). Cassius/Javolenus relies upon the exception introduced by Sabinus in D.19.2.59 : destruction from natural force is a circumstance limiting the builder's general liability for damage to the structure. *Vis aliqua* is surely to be equated with *uis naturalis* or *uis maior* ([18]). But the jurist also restricts the extent to which the employer was liable even for destruction caused by *uis.* He will not bear liability for all destruction caused by force ; he is responsible

(15) M. KASER (cited note 1), 191, on earlier criticisms. I. MOLNÁR (cited note 4), 651, considers the text free of interpolation except (somewhat mysteriously) the expression *si tale.*

(16) R. RÖHLE (cited note 4), 208. O. LENEL, *Paling.* I 277 note 3, and F. SCHULZ, *History* 214, are less confident than Röhle about the authorship of the opinions in many fragments of Javolenus' epitome of Cassius.

(17) The use of the term *detrimentum* in reference to the *locator*'s liability is troublesome to some scholars. J. MIQUEL (cited note 4), 185-186, would prefer to read *periculum* and considers this term a more logical description of the burden of the *locator* with regard to *uis maior.* He attributes this error not to the compilers, but to 'correnti volgari di pensiero' in the post-classical period. However, the two terms are used interchangeably both in this text and by PAUL in D.19.2.62. If a distinction is intended, the vagueness of both terms masks it. They probably do not signify two different types of liability, each appropriate for one of the parties. *Periculum* is used in reference to the party upon whom the chance of loss might fall. *Detrimentum* appears only to mean the monetary loss itself.

(18) There is general agreement on this. The only other occurrence of this phrase is ALFENUS, (2 *dig.*) D.39.2.43 pr. Alfenus declares that an individual is liable to a neighbor under the *cautio damni infecti* if roof tiles are blown off of his house by wind and damage the tiles on his neighbor's roof. But this liability only pertains if the tiles fell off *uitio aedificii* and not because of extraordinary wind or *aliqua ui extrinsecus.* The notion that the force must be out of the control of the owner is strengthened by the addition of *extrinsecus.* Further on this, see D. NÖRR (cited note 12), 116-124.

only if the work would have been approved. This must mean that the employer can be exempt from responsibility if he can demonstrate that the work was not good enough to pass approval.

Röhle interprets the text differently. According to his argument, Cassius assigns *periculum* to an employer who delays in approving the work ([19]). The phrase *si tale opus fuit ut probari deberet* would mean that the work is complete but not yet approved. Cassius therefore agrees with Labeo and defines the contractor's sphere of control broadly in assigning liability before *probatio.* An exception is allowed only if the employer fails in his contractual duties by delaying approval.

This reading is tempting, perhaps because it anticipates Florentinus' rule in D.19.2.36 that the employer is liable for his delay (see below). But Röhle's analysis does not account for the wording of the text. The jurist does not say that the employer bears risk if the work was completed and not approved. He says that the work must have been such (*tale*) as ought to be approved. The wording of the text stresses the *qualitas* of the work and not the stage of completion. The building need not have been complete, but the existing portion must have been sound and in conformity to specifications ([20]). This qualification would protect the employer from suffering loss on a building whose workmanship was faulty. In order to secure a release from liability, the builder probably would have had to prove, or demonstrate to the satisfaction of a *iudex,* that he had executed the contract proficiently according to prevailing standards and in compliance with the specifications.

The rule that the employer bears liability when destruction arises from *uis maior* was accepted in the high classical period. In D.19.2.33, Africanus, citing Julian, draws an analogy from construction law to illustrate a point on liability in tenant farming ([21]). The *locator* has commissioned an *insula* ; a

(19) R. Röhle (cited note 4), 208, argues that the work is so far advanced that it has become the employer's duty to approve it. He may have derived this interpretation from the *Basilica* text (20.1.35 = Heimb. 2.358, Schelt. BT 992 and BS 1198).

(20) *Contra* : C. A. Cannata, *Colpa* 228, argues that *probari debet* could never refer to an unfinished work. Therefore, this case is of theoretical interest but little practical applicability because the *probatio* would become a search through the ruins. But, as J. Miquel (cited note 4), 186, points out, the employer, threatened with a financial loss, would seek assurances that the work had been executed according to specifications. Certainly quite a bit could be determined from an examination of the physical remains.

(21) Africanus, (8 *quaest.*) D.19.2.33 :

> *Si fundus quem mihi locaueris publicatus sit, teneri te actione ex conducto, ut mihi frui liceat, quamuis per te non stet, quo minus id praestes : quemadmodum, inquit, si insulam aedificandam locasses et solum corruisset, nihilo minus teneberis. nam et si uendideris mihi fundum isque priusquam uacuus traderetur publicatus fuerit, tenearis ex empto : quod hactenus uerum erit, ut pretium restituas, non ut etiam id praestes, si quid pluris mea intersit eum uacuum mihi tradi.*

landslide has destroyed it (*solum corruisset*). The *locator* is nevertheless responsible for the payment of *merces*. The analogy apparently serves as an example of the division of liability if *uis maior* disturbs the normal activities of the contract. The source of destruction is similar to that in D.19.2.62, but Africanus does not mention the cause of the soil damage ([22]). He assumes that the collapse of the building site is caused by *uis maior* (this view is supported by the rest of the fragment). Africanus echoes Sabinus' view in D.19.2.59 that destruction resulting from *uis* exempts the builder from liability for failure to complete his job.

A summary of the classical view on the liabilities of the parties is found in a fragment from Florentinus.

> Florentinus, (7 *inst.*) D.19.2.36
>
> *Opus quod auersione locatum est donec adprobetur, conductoris periculum est: quod uero ita conductum sit, ut in pedes mensurasue praestetur, eatenus conductoris periculo est, quatenus admensum non sit: et in utraque causa nociturum locatori, si per eum steterit, quo minus opus adprobetur uel admetiatur. si tamen ui maiore opus prius interciderit quam adprobaretur, locatoris periculo est, nisi si aliud actum sit: non enim amplius praestari locatori oporteat, quam quod sua cura atque opera consecutus esset.*

There has been much comment on this text because it bears clear traces of abbreviation or rewriting, perhaps from the postclassical period ([23]). The fragment falls into four parts, each devoted to a different aspect of the parties' liabilities. I will discuss each part in turn.

The first section (*opus quod-admensum non sit*) specifies that the risk for the structure devolves upon the builder until the building has been approved.

> *similiter igitur et circa conductionem seruandum puto, ut mercedem quam praestiterim restituas, eius scilicet temporis, quo fruitus non fuerim, nec ultra actione ex conducto praestare cogeris. nam et si colonus tuus fundo frui a te aut ab eo prohibetur, quem tu prohibere ne id faciat possis, tantum ei praestabis, quanti eius interfuerit frui, in quo etiam lucrum eius continebitur: sin uero ab eo interpellabitur, quem tu prohibere propter uim maiorem aut potentiam eius non poteris, nihil amplius ei quam mercedem remittere aut reddere debebis.*

On this text, see A. WACKE, *ANRW* II 15 (1976) 455-496 ; H. ANKUM, *SZ* 97 (1980) 157-180 ; P. W. DE NEEVE (cited note 14), 308-318.

(22) The similarity of the factual situations in D.19.2.33 and in D.19.2.15.2 (*labes* = *uis maior*) have contributed to the tendency to analyze *labes* in D.19.2.62 as *uis maior.*

(23) In general on this text, see M. KASER (cited note 1), 192-193 ; J. MIQUEL (cited note 4), 184 ; R. SAMTER, *SZ* 26 (1905) 136-137 ; J. A. C. THOMAS, 685-686 ; C. ALZON (cited note 11), 326-329 ; T. MAYER-MALY, *LC* 40 n. 1 ; C. A. CANNATA, *Colpa* 209-210 ; R. RÖHLE (cited note 4), 209-214 ; M. PIETSCH (cited note 2), 27-31 ; I. MOLNÁR (cited note 4), 654, thinks *donec* is an interpolation. Most scholars read *periculo* in the second line.

This rule can also be inferred from earlier texts, but is stated here in its most complete form. Release from liability occurs after approval if the job was let for a lump sum (*auersione*). The approval of a work let with a price fixed in units of measure (*in pedes mensurasue*) took place at the end of the job when the work was also being measured in order to calculate the final cost. This system is implied in D.19.2.30.3. The parties could choose the method of approval to suit the type of work involved ([24]).

After establishing the broad outlines of the builder's liability for the structure, the text goes on to list circumstances in which the employer assumes liability for harm to the work (*et in utraque-admetiatur*). The employer's position is weakened if he delays in approval of the work. This portion of the text is somewhat troublesome. The participle *nociturum* is without construe, an indication that the text has been abbreviated ([25]). Moreover, the meaning of *nociturum* is not clear. The text does not assign *periculum* to the *locator*, but says that failure to approve will be harmful to him. Normally, the builder would be responsible for any damage done before approval (except in the case of *uis maior*). Evidently, if the building suffered damage while the builder was awaiting approval and final payment of the *merces*, the jurist would permit him to argue that the employer had been dilatory in his approval. But the wording is so vague that it is difficult to evaluate how this would affect the employer's liability except in very general terms. Perhaps the risk for destruction accrued to the employer as his *mora* became apparent. This rule sets an implicit limit to the liability of the builder, who cannot be expected to care continuously for the work once it is completed ([26]).

The next sentence recapitulates the rule on *uis maior* as it developed from Sabinus. The *locator* bears *periculum* for destruction owing to *uis maior* before *probatio*. This is straightforward and, in the absence of any supplementary details, carries us no further than had Africanus. The *nisi*-clause, possibly

(24) On the meaning of the terms *auersione* and *in pedes mensurasue*, see S. Martin, *SZ* 103 (1986) 321-337, with earlier bibliography, and below at Chapter III, section D.

(25) On this, see especially R. Röhle (cited note 4), 209-210, who concludes that *nociturum* is the remnant of an omitted citation, a result of post-classical abbreviation. On the transmission of the *Institutes*, see F. Schulz, *History* 158-159. The text is certainly abbreviated. J. A. C. Thomas, 685, interprets this phrase very precisely as denying the *conductor* an *id quod interest* payment from the *locator* who would only have to pay *merces* or part of it.

(26) M. Pietsch (cited note 2), 44-50, establishes this sentence as the sole indication of a *tempus probationis*, the time allotted the employer for completion of the *probatio*. This is, of course, not conclusive evidence for the existence of a fixed *tempus probationis*, see below my analysis of D.19.2.24 pr. at Chapter III, section C.

a later addition, provides for the alteration of this arrangement through a clause in the contract ([27]).

The last phrase presents something of an enigma and is usually considered interpolated ([28]). The words *non enim* seem to offer a rationale for the preceding sentence, but this collocation of phrases produces an awkward and unintelligible conclusion to the text. The final sentence must translate roughly as follows : "for the *locator* ought not to gain more than what he would have obtained by his own care and work". This statement does not develop logically from the preceding discussion of the rule on *uis maior* which assigns responsibility to the *locator.* The last phrase seems better intended as an explanation of the earlier sentence, wherein the *locator* is made liable for his delay in approving the work. In this case, it can rightly be determined that the employer should not receive recompense above that obtained by his own effort. If he delays in approving the work, he cannot expect that the builder will be responsible for damage or loss for an indeterminate period of time. The text has undergone some post-classical abbreviation or reworking. Perhaps the statement on *uis maior* was inserted into the text in order to give a complete summary of the employer's responsibility to the builder. The last phrase was retained as a general explanation of the limitation on his liability. If this analysis is acceptable, it would probably be better to punctuate differently and change the colon after *actum sit* to a period. This would diminish the tendency to read the end as closely connected with the previous phrase ([29]).

As Pietsch and others have pointed out, this text has the earmarks of a handbook and summarizes guidelines current in the jurists' law at that time ([30]). This type of summary provided the parties with an objective statement of their expectations as they entered into construction contracts. As we can see, the builder has a generalized responsibility for the condition of the work until *probatio.* The few limitations have resulted from cases

(27) See M. KASER (cited note 1), 192-193 and n. 146. The *nisi*-clause is universally rejected.

(28) C. A. CANNATA, *Colpa* 209, would eliminate this phrase altogether. T. MAYER-MALY, *LC* 40, reads *conductor* as the subject of *consecutus,* but this seems strained ; R. RÖHLE (cited note 4), 212, also prefers that *cura* and *opera* refer to the activity of the *conductor.*

(29) E. BETTI (cited note 4), 15, rewrites the phrase and connects these two phrases more closely: *si tamen ui naturali opus prius interciderit quam adprobaretur, locatoris periculo est, maxime si in mora fuit, cum non amplius praestari locatori oporteat, quam quod tunc consecutus esset.* He is correct in seeing that these statements are logically connected. It is probably not valid to suppose that the employer's *mora* only affects his *periculum* for *uis maior.*

(30) M. PIETSCH (cited note 2), 29.

regarding the employer's delay in approving, or in the case of destruction from *uis maior.*

Paul's comment on Labeo in D.19.2.62 is the final statement about the division of *periculum* in building contracts. The response indicates that Labeo's conception of each party's sphere of control has undergone modification in the intervening centuries. The employer bears *periculum* for damage arising from *uitium soli,* the builder, for *uitium operis* ([31]). This opinion offers a more complex and differentiated view of division of risk than that implied in Labeo's response. Labeo had considered the builder responsible for damage to the building site which occurred in the course of construction. This liability was implicit in the obligation and did not look to the cause of the damage as an essential fact in determining liability. In D.19.2.59, Sabinus created an important limitation in case of *uis maior.* Paul's category of *uitium soli* is the final step in the direction of limiting the builder's liability : he shifts on to the employer the burden for damage to the structure arising from the site. The question of foreseeability as a factor in determining liability is not discussed explicitly, and *uitium soli* may apply to any fault in the soil which could not be reasonably foreseen by the builder. Thus the outcome of D.19.2.62, in which the landslide had occurred as a direct result of the construction, may not have been changed by Paul's differentiation of the employer's liability.

The phrase *uitium operis* encompasses the builder's duty to warrant his skilled completion of the job. He is responsible for all facets of the work : organization, execution and supervision. This responsibility is later tested in the process of approval. The fact that this text discusses allotment of *periculum* does not restrict the discussion to risk arising from accidental events. The phrase *uitium operis* broadens the scope of *periculum* by including the builder's primary responsibility which was to build ([32]). The duty to produce

(31) No convincing objections have been advanced concerning the classicity of this decision. The strident, almost condescending tone is characteristic of Paul's epitome of the *Pithana.* See especially J. A. C. Thomas in A. Watson, ed., *Daube Noster : Essays in Legal History for David Daube* (1974) 317-325. M. Kaser (cited note 1), 188-189, finds Paul's comment so abbreviated as to be almost incomprehensible. Still, he is not willing to consider it the creation of a post-classical epitomator.

(32) M. Kaser (cited note 1), 189, maintained that *uitium operis* pertained only to events arising from accidents and not to faulty behavior of the builder. He later altered this view, *RPR*^{2} I 571 n. 91. The tendency to restrict the craftsman's liability to include only his area of expertise is found in other areas of *locatio conductio operis,* for example, D.19.2.13.5 (*gemma includenda aut insculpenda*), D.9.2.27.29 (*calicem diatretum faciendum*), D.19.2.9.5 (*uitulos pascendos uel sarciendum quid poliendumue*).

the *opus* may, however, also have required him to be responsible for reasonably foreseeable consequences of his work in regard to the building site. The builder could not, for example, undertake a job in the knowledge that the site was weak and expect the employer to bear the full financial burden when the structure collapsed.

Paul's division of the parties' spheres of control into these two categories presumably altered the way in which litigants approached their cases. Henceforth, instead of relying upon reasoning by analogy from case to case, they would attempt to fit the facts into one of the two categories, which would in turn be tested and developed by the addition of new cases and factual situations.

Stipulation and damage during construction

As we have seen, the jurisprudence devoted to *periculum* in *locatio conductio operis* relies upon the ideas of implicit spheres of control. The parties, even at the outset of the contract, are encouraged to assume that some duties and obligations are accepted as part of the obligation. Therefore, in certain cases, the jurists will not enforce the builder's obligation strictly, but will limit his liability according to factors such as good faith, fault and other mitigating factors. These limitations become part of the contour of each party's overall responsibility under the contract.

One text dealing with a contract for construction in *stipulatio* presents a factual situation similar to those discussed above : the building is destroyed before the completion and discharge of the contractor's obligation. The manner in which the jurist handles the builder's liability in this case furnishes a point of comparison between stipulation and *locatio* in terms of the expectations and duties imposed by the obligation.

> Pomponius, (27 *ad Sab.*) D.45.1.15
>
> *Et ideo haesitatur, si aliqua pars insulae facta sit, deinde incendio consumpta sit, an integrum tempus computandum sit rursus ad aedificandam insulam an uero reliquum dumtaxat exspectandum quod deerat. et uerius est, ut integrum ei detur.*

The text is sound ([33]). A fire has interrupted the progress of a builder who has contracted through *stipulatio* to build an *insula.* The structure, which was only partially complete, has probably been destroyed although the extent of the damage is not made clear. Pomponius is asked whether the builder

(33) R. Röhle (cited note 4), 204-205 ; C. A. Cannata, *Colpa* 159 and 234-236.

should be expected to fulfill his obligation within the time remaining under the terms of the agreement ; the text proposes as an alternative to this the allotment of the *integrum tempus*, the full contract term, either a specified period or the implied 'reasonable time', in which to rebuild the structure.

It is clear from the text that the stipulator wishes to hold the builder to the original agreement despite the obvious hindrance imposed by the fire. The builder is resisting the idea that he must complete the work to term. The consequences of enforcing the original deadline would be disastrous : he would not be able to finish on time, and this would result in penalties for delay in addition to the expense of rebuilding the *insula*. Pomponius thinks that a more correct approach to this dilemma is to allow the promissor the full contract term all over again. But this view was controversial as the language of the text indicates (*ideo haesitatur ; uerius est*). Some jurists would argue in favor of interpreting the contract strictly in favor of the stipulator.

Pomponius gives us no reason why his decision should be more correct. Presumably the basis for his opinion lies in the fact that a fire is the cause of the potential delay, and the builder's lack of fault influences the outcome of the case. In general, the law on *stipulatio* tended to uphold the agreement strictly as it was formulated by the parties. Pomponius is willing to extend the contract term against the explicit content of the agreement, but his decision is narrowly conceived. The fact that the problem of destruction during the contract term is discussed in terms of extending the completion date tells us something about the relationship created by stipulation. There is no reliance upon implicit terms or spheres of control as in *locatio conductio*. The jurist makes no attempt to generalize or to introduce a category of exceptional events such as *uis maior* ([34]). The builder's only hope is in a time extension granted as an exception. From this point of view, stipulation could be risky for the builder : even if the jurists were willing to allow more time for the completion of the structure on the grounds that the accident was not his fault, he still would have to bear the added expenses of rebuilding the burned portion of the *insula*.

(34) On the distinct methods of interpretation used in *stipulatio* and *locatio*, see R. RÖHLE (cited note 4), 205, who rightly stresses the differences between the two contracts. It seems unlikely that the roots of the practice in *locatio conductio* were to be found in the law on *stipulatio operis faciendi* as V. ARANGIO-RUIZ, *Resp.* 189 n. 1, supposed.

SECTION C
PROBATIO OPERIS

Probatio operis, the final approval of the work, is a crucial moment for both builder and employer ([1]). The builder submits the work to the employer for inspection ; he examines the structure (or has it examined) and measures the sufficiency of the builder's work. *Probatio* seems to have been well established by the second century B.C. in public law, and numerous inscriptions attest the early practice of designating magistrates as approvers of public projects ([2]). In general, a contract was sold at auction by a municipal or state official ; censors are the most commonly attested, but consuls, aediles and urban praetors at Rome, and *duouiri* and *duouirales* elsewhere, administered contracts for public works ([3]). A clause in the contract named the officials who were to approve the work, and, as is the case in the *lex parieti faciundo Puteolana*, these individuals were not necessarily the same magistrates who had let the contract initially ([4]).

The job of the magistrate in charge was to grant *probatio* or *improbatio* after an inspection of the job ([5]). The contractor's final payment depended in principle upon the successful outcome of *probatio*, as the contract from

(1) Despite the relative importance of *probatio* in both public and private construction law, literature on the topic is not abundant, see R. SAMTER, *SZ* 26 (1905) 125-144, and M. PIETSCH, *Die Abnahme im Werkvertragsrecht* (diss. Hamburg, 1976) 23-55. J. A. C. THOMAS, 673-689, and C. A. CANNATA, *Colpa* 133-240, discuss *probatio* in regard to building contracts ; see also S. MARTIN, *SZ* 103 (1986) 321-337.

(2) A. BISCARDI, *St.Sen.* 72 (1960) 433-434, collects the epigraphic sources on *probatio.* See also P. A. BRUNT, *JRS* 70 (1980) 85 n. 16. The only really informative epigraphic source is the *lex parieti faciundo Puteolana* (*FIRA* III # 153 = *ILLRP* 518). On this see T. WIEGAND, 660-778. *Probatio* seems well developed already by 105 B.C., as the *lex Puteolana* indicates ; in private law, the practice is implied by CATO *Agr.* 144.

(3) Consul : *CIL* I² 694 ; Aedile : *CIL* I² 1560 ; *ILLRP* 449 ; Censors : LIVY 45.15.9 ; Praetor : CIC. 2 *Verr.* i.130. *Duouiri* and *duouirales* : *FIRA* III # 153 = *ILLRP* 518 ; cf. *FIRA* I # 24 = *ILS* 6089 (*lex municipii Malacitani*) c. 63.

(4) See E. BADIAN, *Publicans and Sinners* (1972) 31 n. 18. The *lex Puteolana* authorizes a group of *duouiri* and *duouirales* to vote on approval : at least twenty must be present when the approval is voted ; no fewer than twenty must vote in favor of the approver for it to succeed. See T. WIEGAND, 680-682.

(5) *Improbatio* is commonly used to indicate a failure to gain approval. On the terminology used in *probatio*, see R. SAMTER (cited note 1), 125-130 ; M. PIETSCH (cited note 1), 37 ; R. RÖHLE, *SD* 34 (1965) 206. For an example of *improbatio*, see below at D.19.2.60.3 and CIC. *Font.* 8.17-18.

Puteoli suggests (6). Ideally, the assiduous magistrate attempted to discern how skillfully and carefully the builder had followed his orders. There was, however, room for discretion in determining the quality of the construction, and charges of corruption arose occasionally (7). The only detailed account of magisterial *probatio* comes from Cicero's version of Verres' supervision of the maintenance contract for the temple of Castor and Pollux, probably a typical example except for the corrupt way in which it was administered (8).

The contract for the upkeep of the *aedes Castoris* had been held by P. Iunius since 80. After Iunius' death, one of his son's tutors, Habonius, was to assume the contract (131-132). As part of this transfer, the Praetor conducted an approval of the temple and if he discovered any faults or irregularities, he could require Iunius' estate to pay for the repairs. According to Cicero, Verres found that the temple was in excellent condition. Nevertheless, on the advice of one of his followers, he ordered the younger Iunius and his guardians to have the columns made plumb (*columnae ad perpendiculum exigantur*), a requirement belittled by Cicero as both absurd and not specified in the original contract (132-134). The guardians, after fruitless attempts at personal persuasion, paid for a new repair contract (140-142). Verres delayed approving this contract until four years after it had been let despite a proviso in the terms that the work be done within a matter of months (148-149). This is an extreme example, of course, but points out the dangers to builders in public contracting when the magistrate has complete discretion over the interpretation of the contract. Private law contracts were less risky because the builder could initiate an *actio conducti* if he felt the employer's approval had been arbitrarily conducted. However, there was no guarantee that the judge would sustain the contractor's interpretation of his execution of the obligation (9).

Although there is no full description in private law of the workings of *probatio*, much of the standard procedure can be reconstructed from *Digest*

(6) *FIRA* III # 153 = *ILLRP* 518 : *dies pequn(iae) : pars dimidia dabitur ubei praedia satis subsignata erunt, altera pars dimidia soluetur opere effecto probatoque.*

(7) See Cic. *Font.* 8.17-18, on the charges alleged against M. Fonteius that he profited from public contracts for the construction of roads partly by accepting bribes in return for which he would overlook faulty construction.

(8) Cic. 2 *Verr.* i 130-150. See E. Badian (cited note 4), 31 n. 18. References to specific passages are incorporated into the text.

(9) R. Samter (cited note 1), 124-127, assumed a direct influence of public law upon *probatio* as it was carried out in private law. On this, see S. Martin (cited note 1), 322-324. There is no evidence for this development ; it seems equally likely that the practice originated in private contracts.

texts. *Probatio* consisted of an examination of the structure either by the *locator* himself or by his heir. The heir could conduct *probatio* as the successor of the *locator* (D.19.2.60.3 ; 19.2.24 pr.). It is also conceivable that landowners designated a third party, such as an architect, to accomplish approval and engaged this person through the contract of mandate ([10]). The builder submitted his work for inspection (*adprobare*, D.19.2.36), and it was either approved (*probatio*) or not (*improbatio*, D.19.2.60.3). The approval took place at the end of the term and released the builder from further responsibility for the structure unless he had obtained the approval fraudulently (D.19.2.24 pr.). If the job had been let with a price calculated in units of measure (*in pedes mensurasue*), the approval took place at the same time as final measurement, which determined the total price for the work (D.19.2.30.3) ([11]). The goal of *probatio* was to ascertain the soundness and quality of the construction and its conformity to specifications (D.19.2.60.3 ; 19.2.51.1). If the work was faulty or did not conform to the contract, the builder then repaired the work at his own expense. If, however, the builder felt that his work was acceptable, he might prefer to initiate an action.

It seems likely that the employer made periodic inspections of the work in a supervisory way during the term of the contract. A passage in the correspondence of Cicero illustrates the early stages of a *probatio* ([12]). In a letter to his brother Quintus, Cicero details his inspection of a villa being built or refurbished on one of Quintus' country estates. Cicero systematically examines the work of the builder Diphilus and orders changes where necessary. At one point he simply remarks that certain vaulted ceilings are unsuitable and must be changed (*non probaui*) ; in the case of a colonnade, however, he spots bad workmanship and requires Diphilus to pull down the columns and do them again ([13]). In a typical building contract, the approval may have been conducted in this manner, both in periodic inspections and at the end. An early inspection would avoid a disastrous final *improbatio* when changes would be harder to make. There was also less likelihood that an action would result if the landowner worked closely with the builder.

(10) The jurists give no specific examples of this, and it is only a matter of speculation that architects were hired in this way. It seems to have been common to have supervisory personnel overseeing the job, and they may have had the right to approve, see chapter II.

(11) For a fuller discussion of this, see below at Chapter III, section D.

(12) Cic. *Q.fr.* 3.1.1-2.

(13) Cic. *Q.fr.* 3.1.1 : *Cameras quasdam non probaui, mutarique iussi* ; 3.1.2 : *Columnas neque rectas, neque e regione Diphilus collocarat. eas scilicet demolietur.*

Periodic supervision was not required and did not affect the builder's responsibility for the condition of the building upon completion ([14]).

As we have seen, the employer's right to approve a structure built under *locatio conductio operis* was established in public law by the end of the second century B.C. In private contracts, the first explicit testimony is in a text from Alfenus (3 *dig. a Paulo epit.*, D.19.2.30.3). Most of the sources assume that either the employer or a specifically designated surrogate will conduct the approval, and in general, a contract clause named the person charged with this task. This practice is attested in the public law sources in the second century B.C., and most privately concluded contracts presumably contained the name of an approver. In one case, however, Javolenus discusses an unusual factual situation which has led to a confrontation between the parties concerning the responsibility of the builder to guarantee the quality of the work in *probatio.*

> Javolenus, (11 *epit.*) D.19.2.51.1
>
> *Locaui opus faciendum ita, ut pro opere redemptori certam mercedem in dies singulos darem : opus uitiosum factum est : an ex locato agere possim ? respondit : si ita opus locasti, ut bonitas eius tibi a conductore adprobaretur, tametsi conuenit, ut in singulas operas certa pecunia daretur, praestari tamen tibi a conductore debet, si id opus uitiosum factum est : non enim quicquam interest, utrum uno pretio opus an in singulas operas collocatur, si modo uniuersitas consummationis ad conductorem pertinuit. poterit itaque ex locato cum eo agi, qui uitiosum opus fecerit. nisi si ideo in operas singulas merces constituta erit, ut arbitrio domini opus efficeretur : tum enim nihil conductor praestare domino de bonitate operis uidetur.*

The text has been abbreviated, but the substance is probably classical ([15]). The case involves a contract let with the provision that the contractor receive his pay in daily sums. When the work turns out to be faulty, the employer asks whether he can bring an *actio locati* against the contractor on the grounds that the work fails to meet his approval.

Javolenus' response raises an extremely important issue for the parties to a construction contract in *locatio* : is the employer justified in assuming that the builder has a duty to be responsible to him for the quality of the work ?

(14) Speculation about the possibility of an interim or step-by-step *probatio* has caused a great deal of misunderstanding, see below at Chapter III, section D.

(15) The text is probably sound through the word *collocatur.* The most serious objections have been raised against the last sentence (*nisi si – fin*), see below at note 17. For a fuller discussion, see S. Martin (cited note 1), 330-332.

The contract apparently lacks a specific reference to the employer's intention to conduct final approval. The builder is alleging that the allotment of pay *in dies singulos,* clearly an uncommon arrangement in a contract to fabricate a building (*opus faciendum*), indicates that he did not agree to be responsible for the quality of the finished product. Indeed, the builder may be trying to argue that the contract price was expressed in terms of daily sums because his job was to provide a certain amount of labor : the employer did not intend to hold him responsible for the whole project. If he could prove his case, he would not be liable for final approval of the job ([16]). The use of the phrase *in dies singulos* to designate the contract price has created an ambiguity, and the employer seeks a resolution from the jurist.

Javolenus carefully emphasizes the relative unimportance of the method of payment when weighed against the original intention of the employer in agreeing to the terms. If the contract was formed with the intention of hiring a builder who would be responsible for quality, then the builder was liable. The designation of payment in daily sums does not automatically determine liability by implying a daily release from responsibility. The jurist dismisses the possibility that the builder's claim was justified, and upholds the employer's interpretation of the contract.

In the last sentence, however, Javolenus suggests a hypothetical situation in which the fee had been fixed in daily sums specifically because the owner wanted to supervise the work closely ([17]). The builder would not be responsible for quality in this case. The jurist introduces this counter-example in order to emphasize the importance of the employer's intent in establishing the extent of the builder's responsibility. The result of this decision is that a contract for a job of work can include an unusual payment schedule without this detail offering presumptive evidence concerning the builder's liability for *probatio.* A lump sum payment probably indicated that the contract was for fabrication of a whole project, and therefore implied *probatio* at the end. But

(16) The builder may be trying to claim that he was hired on an arrangement such as *locatio conductio operarum,* a contract for daily labor. Under this contract, the *locator,* who leases his *operae,* appears to lose his right to payment if it is his fault that the work is not done, D.19.2.38 pr.-1, see M. Kaser, *RPR*[2] I 568-570. A. Berger, *CP* 43 (1948) 231-242, on *FIRA* III # 150, notes that the worker is hired simply to work ; there is no liability for *imperitia.* The only express requirement placed upon the worker is that he be sound in body.

(17) This hypothetical case is poorly expressed and is thought by some to deny the solution proposed earlier in the text. See C. A. Cannata, *Colpa* 211-212 ; E. Alberario, *APer.* 31 (1919) 51 n. 2 and 25. I. Molnár, *ANRW* II 14 (1982) 655-656 and n. 255, argues that the last sentence was added as clarification by the compilers and does not alter the essentially classical content of the text.

in the case of other arrangements, such as a daily wage, mere payment does not imply release from liability.

If the employer chose to bring an action based upon *improbatio*, the arguments on each side would involve assessments of technical skill and conformity to specifications. The primary evidence for the specifications was the contract itself, provided that there was a written copy of it. In some instances, however, the jurists were also willing to consider evidence external to the content of the agreement which would mitigate against a strict interpretation of the content of the contract.

Labeo, (5 *post. a Iau. epit.*) D.19.2.60.3

Lege dicta domus facienda locata erat ita, ut probatio aut improbatio locatoris aut heredis eius esset : redemptor ex uoluntate locatoris quaedam in opere permutauerat. respondi opus quidem ex lege dicta non uideri factum, sed quoniam ex uoluntate locatoris permutatum esset, redemptorem absolui debere.

The text has never been considered seriously interpolated ([18]). The use of the first person (*respondi*) and the inscription indicate that the response is Labeo's ([19]). The contract contains a *lex locationis* providing that the employer or his heir conduct the *probatio* or *improbatio*. During the course of construction, the builder makes some alterations in the specifications (*quaedam in opere permutauerat*) at the behest of the employer. Later, an *actio locati* is brought based upon the contractor's alleged non-performance *ex lege dicta*, as a direct result of the alterations.

The case and the situation underlying it raise several interesting points. First, the text implies that the contract contains explicit specifications for the work. Secondly, the approval may fail because certain aspects of the work are non-conforming ; the construction need not be poorly executed, or fail totally to correspond with the *leges locationis*. Third, the emphasis upon the heir's right to conduct the *probatio* may derive from the underlying factual situation : the employer has died, and his heir, upon observing the alteration in the work, has initiated an action against the contractor ([20]).

(18) Only G. Beseler, *SZ* 57 (1937) 41, thinks *aut improbatio* is objectionable. *Contra* : M. Kaser, *St. Biondi* I (1965) 122 n. 158 ; 133 n. 273.

(19) The *Basilica* text attributes the opinion to Labeo by name (20.1.60.3 = Heimb. 2.366, Schelt. BT 996 and BS 1206). See F. Schulz, *History* 207-208 ; P. Jörs, *RE* s.v. Antistius # 34 col. 2548-2557 (1894).

(20) R. Samter (cited note 1), 140 n. 1. F. Horak, *Rationes decidendi* I (1969) 212, also argues that it is the heir who brings the action ; but see L. Amirante, *Bull.* 62 (1959) 84, who thinks that the employer brought the action because the work did not correspond to the 'ideal' work envisioned in the contract.

Labeo releases the builder from any liability for the non-conformity of the work, but concedes that from a technical point of view the plaintiff's claims are well-grounded : the work does not correspond to the specifications of the contract. This statement implies that evidence of the original specifications remains. Labeo accepts the builder's evidence of a subsequent alteration in the terms, even though the changes were probably made orally and therefore could not be verified. If the heir is actually the litigant, he may have been ignorant of the employer's changes ; alternatively, he may have been aware of them, but preferred the original specifications. Through the *actio locati* he sought to enforce the initial agreement. Labeo's interpretation relies essentially upon good faith. Since the contractor carried out the wishes of the employer in good faith, he cannot be made liable for deviating from the terms of the contract in order to implement the specific changes requested by the employer.

The execution of *probatio* involved the employer in an examination of a rather technical nature. Not only was he able to condemn aspects of the building which failed to suit his taste and expectations, he was also passing upon the soundness of the structure itself. In any building project, perfection is unattainable, and there is a large grey area between precise, high-quality work and an unacceptably poor execution of the specifications. A major issue in deciding cases was how far the employer's opinion of the construction was to be taken as a standard for judging the builder's liability. Paul suggests one way in which these disputes could be handled :

> Paul, (34 *ad ed.*) D.19.2.24 pr.
>
> *Si in lege locationis comprehensum sit, ut arbitratu domini opus adprobetur, perinde habetur, ac si uiri boni arbitrium comprehensum fuisset, idemque seruatur, si alterius cuiuslibet arbitrium comprehensum sit : nam fides bona exigit, ut arbitrium tale praestetur, quale uiro bono conuenit. idque arbitrium ad qualitatem operis, non ad prorogandum tempus, quod lege finitum sit, pertinet, nisi id ipsum lege comprehensum sit. quibus consequens est, ut irrita sit adprobatio dolo conductoris facta, ut ex locato agi possit.*

The text is generally thought to be sound (21). Paul summarizes the duties of both parties in conducting *probatio.* In the first section (through *quale uiro*

(21) See M. Pietsch (cited note 1), 40-41 ; C. A. Cannata, *Colpa* 198 and 206-207 ; T. Mayer-Maly, *LC* 111-112 n. 31, with bibliography. These scholars have refuted the earlier suspicions advanced by E. Albertario, *Studi di diritto Romano* III (1936) 285-310, concerning this text and several others on the grounds that neither the *dominus* nor any other party to the contract could have the right of *arbitrium* over the fulfillment.

bono conuenit), he interprets a contract clause assigning to the owner, who is also the *locator*, the task of approving the work. The response examines what it means when we say that the landowner is to have the *arbitrium* and answers the underlying question : is the *arbitrium* absolute or is it limited in any way ?

Paul responds that the owner's evaluation of the work must correspond to an *arbitrium boni uiri*, the judgment of a good man. He extends this opinion to apply to any third party to whom the owner has entrusted this task. This conclusion, he says, relies upon the requirements of good faith which dictate a standard for measuring the *arbitrium*. He infers from the good faith nature of the contract the requirement that the employer's evaluation be limited in its scope to correspond to what a good man would find reasonable ([22]).

In developing the use of the 'good man' standard, which was already known to Cato, Paul was grappling with one of the main difficulties in conducting *probatio* : the *arbitrium*, or determination of quality, requires that decisions on matters of technical skill be made by individuals who often had little expertise in building ([23]). Moreover, the employer, or his representative, desires to obtain the maximum amount of work from the contractor and to approximate as closely as possible the perfect execution of the plan before releasing him from further responsibility. At a certain point, the interests of the employer were sure to conflict with those of the builder, who had to worry about the likelihood that, even in the absence of outright bad workmanship, his work was unlikely to be a perfect manifestation of the architect's plan.

In this text, Paul establishes that the employer's opinion cannot be the sole standard used in measuring the contractor's performance. The use of the *arbitrium uiri boni* broadens the range of evidence which can be considered in the evaluation of the work to include such factors as standards prevalent in the trade. Here, as elsewhere, the jurists demonstrate a familiarity with the concerns of building. As we have seen, in D.45.1.137.2-3, Venuleius suggests

(22) On the use of the *arbitrium boni uiri*, see M. KASER, *RPR*^{2} I 490 n. 23 ; P. VOCI, *Le obbligazioni romane* I i (1969) 190-204. On Paul and the application of the *arbitrium boni uiri*, see also D.17.2.76-79 and F. GALLO, *Studi in onore di G. Grosso* III (1970) 534-540, who considers this technique an assessment conducted according to 'criteri correnti'.

(23) CATO *Agr.* 144, uses similar terminology in assigning a right to approve either to the *locator* or to his *custos* ; see P. THIELSCHER, *Des Marcus Cato Belehrung über die Landwirtschaft* (1963) 343-344, on the similarity between Cato and Paul in this text ; see also U. VON LÜBTOW, *Symbolae Raphaeli Taubenschlag dedicatae* III (1957) = *Eos* 48.3 (1956) 437-441.

that a 'good man' standard involves an investigation of current practices in building. In another context, Ulpian, (1 *ad ed. aed.*) D.21.1.19.4, asserts that those called *artifices* need not be highly qualified in order to accept employment. They must be skilled only to the degree commonly held acceptable in their trade ([24]). Underlying the use of the *arbitrium boni uiri* is the supposition that information about prevalent standards is available, and indeed the very use of this technique may have been predicated upon the fact that it was possible to determine adequate levels of skill by consulting specialists in the trade. Paul avoids involving juristic law in the technical aspects of approval, which are questions of fact. He establishes the guideline, but the actual work of determining the quality devolved upon the *iudex* on a case-by-case basis. While a certain set of standards, or at least reasonable expectations, may have grown up over time from decisions granted on actions, a great deal of discretion was allowed the *iudex* in deciding individual cases.

In the next section of the text (*idque arbitrium-comprehensum sit*), Paul limits the scope of the *arbitrium* to apply only to the suitability of the work (*qualitas*) and not to an extension of the time limit fixed in a contract clause. The *iudex* is thereby instructed to limit his use of the 'good man' standard to the employer's evaluation in *probatio.* Gauging *qualitas* is the purpose of approval ; both quality of workmanship and conformity to the contract clauses are to be examined ([25]). The admonition not to use the *arbitrium* to extend the *tempus quod lege finitum sit* undoubtedly refers to the term of the contract. There is no reason to infer from this phrase a *tempus probationis,* a period of time within which the approval must occur. No source explicitly refers to a *lex locationis* setting an approval date ([26]). Of course it was normal for the parties to include a *lex locationis* naming the date set for completion. Paul wishes to keep separate the problems of quality control (determined through *probatio*) and delay. While the contractor can expect questions of skill and conformity to be reviewed with reference to *bona fides,* the time limit will remain fixed. The *iudex* is under no compulsion to judge the

(24) On VENULEIUS, (1 *stip.*) D.45.1.137.2-3, see above at Chapter III, section A.

(25) On the meaning of *qualitas,* see P. CORNIOLEY, *St. Grosso* II (1968) 251-295. The word often denotes characteristic features or substance rather than quality ('goodness'). Of course *qualitas,* in the sense of conformity to specifications, also involved the level of skill to be used.

(26) The *tempus probationis* originated with R. SAMTER (cited note 1), 127-128, and is restated by C. A. CANNATA, *Colpa* 204-207. Both J. A. C. THOMAS, 688, and M. PIETSCH (cited note 1), 44-48, offer limitations to Samter's view. There are no examples of this clause.

fairness of a term to which both parties agreed at the outset. The employer has the capacity to grant a time extension if he wishes to do so ([27]).

The *nisi*-clause, possibly a later addition, does not affect my interpretation. It may simply establish that the parties are free to attach a *lex* permitting the contractor to seek an extension of the time limit through the *arbitrium* of the magistrate. No other evidence suggests that clauses of this type were normal features of construction contracts. However, an implicit time limit is established in D.19.2.36. Florentinus says that damage to the structure before approval will be at the risk of the employer if he has delayed in his approval, suggesting that a normal approval would proceed relatively rapidly after the completion of the work, which was in the interest of the builder since he remained responsible for the condition of the building until it was approved ([28]).

The last sentence (*quibus consequens-agi possit*) views *probatio* from another perspective ([29]). Paul has thus far concerned himself with the constraints placed by *bona fides* upon the employer's influence over approval. In this last phrase, he considers the duty placed upon the contractor by good faith. If the contractor obtains *probatio* through *dolus*, the approval is void, and the employer can bring an *actio locati.* This rule fixes *probatio* as the moment when the builder's liability for correcting faults ceases. In an *actio locati* at the time of *probatio*, the employer must only prove that faults exist. Thereafter, he must accept all faults he discovers unless he can demonstrate that the contractor had not acted in good faith during the approval. This rule encourages both parties to participate actively in the evaluation to insure that

(27) This is implied in D.45.1.113 pr., see Chapter III, section D.

(28) The portion of the text from *nisi si-comprehensum sit* has been criticized, see C. A. CANNATA, *Colpa* 207, and F. EISELE, *SZ* 10 (1889) 311. On the possibility that the *nisi*-clause is sound, see M. PIETSCH (cited note 1), 45 n. 113, and in general A. BERGER (cited note 16). D.19.2.36 implies that the *locator* is penalized for delaying his approval. Cf. CIC. 2 *Verr.* i 149, on the extraordinary four-year wait for approval. For an instructive parallel from Greek law, see A. BURFORD, *The Greek Temple Builders at Epidauros* (1969) 98, on a clause in a public contract from Delos outlining the procedure of approval and specifying that the work had to be inspected within ten days, after which time the responsibility for faults reverted to the building commission. This is in a sense a *tempus probationis*, but, as in D.19.2.36, the intention is to accomplish the approval quickly.

(29) On the use of the word *consequens* in the *Digest,* see W. WALDSTEIN, *SZ* 92 (1975) 26-68 ; F. HORAK, *Fs. Kaser* (1978) 29-56. V. ARANGIO-RUIZ, *Resp.* 200, considered the last phrase (*ut ex locato agi possit*) interpolated on the grounds that it is awkward and omits the inevitable step of a new *probatio.* However, it seems unlikely that a new *probatio* was required ; the *locator* would only be interested in trying to demonstrate the builder's bad faith through the *actio locati.* See also R. RÖHLE (cited note 5), 206-207. I would like to thank the *Thesaurus Linguae Latinae* for furnishing references to *probatio.*

the employer is aware of all aspects of the structure. *Dolus* must have usually involved any attempt to conceal features of construction in such a way that the inspector came away with an exaggerated opinion of its quality.

In this regard, the question of latent defects is of considerable interest. What if, after two years, major structural damage appears as a result of some defect not readily detectable at the time of approval ? The texts indicate that the employer had no remedy for this damage unless he could prove that the contractor knew about the defects and concealed them. This opinion enhances the importance of *probatio* as the employer's last chance to detect faults in the work and demonstrates the jurists' unwillingness to extend the obligation beyond the convenient limit of approval.

SECTION D

PAYMENT AND PAYMENT PROBLEMS

As we have seen, provisions for the builder's *merces* were included as one of the requirements for the formation of the contract (1). The payment he receives constitutes his main interest in the contract and from this he normally derives his livelihood. Because very little is known about the costs of private building projects or the payment of builders, it is impossible to calculate how much a builder might expect to earn from a typical project once his expenses for labor, machinery and materials were deducted from the *merces* (2).

When a suit arose in *locatio conductio operis*, the dispute involved the builder's right to the *merces* in full which the employer sought to withhold. In general, the builder did not receive full payment until the moment of final *probatio* when all responsibility for the structure was transferred to the employer. After this point, the builder's obligation was complete ; he received the full contract price and had no further liability except in the case of his *dolus*. Therefore, the two events, payment and *probatio*, were closely linked. If the price was fixed in a lump sum, the builder usually received payment in two installments, half at the beginning and half when the work was completed and approved (3). But the contract could admit a variety of arrangements, for example, *merces* calculated in daily allotments, a practice which was evidently not common (4).

The relationship between final payment and approval is made explicit by Florentinus in D.19.2.36 where he refers to two standard methods of formulating the *merces* in the contract : *auersione*, calculation of *merces* in a lump sum, and *in pedes mensurasue*, provision for payment by unit of

(1) See Chapter I.

(2) R. Duncan-Jones, *The Economy of the Roman Empire*² (1982) 124-125 and 157-160, reviews Italian building costs. These prices are usually for the construction or maintenance of large structures, such as baths or basilicas, or for road construction. Many of the costs we have from Roman antiquity are from inscriptions recording private munificence in the form of funds for constructing or remodeling a public building, see B. Ward-Perkins, *From Classical Antiquity to the Middle Ages* (1984) 3-37.

(3) This practice seems to have been standard, see Cic. *Q.Fr.* 2.4.2, Labeo, D.19.2.60.4 (cited below) and the *lex Puteolana, FIRA* III # 153 = *ILLRP* 518.

(4) Javolenus, D.19.2.51.1, refers to a contract with the payment specified *in dies singulos*, see above at Chapter III, section C.

measure (5). Florentinus goes on to state that while contracts with *merces* in a lump sum (*auersione*) are discharged through *probatio*, those with payment *in pedes mensurasue* are approved by measurement.

The most commonly accepted interpretation of this text has emphasized the distinction between these two terms in defining the builder's liability for overall quality : *auersione* indicates a final approval of the work as a whole ; *in pedes mensurasue* calls for approval in steps as the work progressed (6). The second method would not entail an overall responsibility for the quality of the job. As I have explained elsewhere, this interpretation may be based upon a misreading of Florentinus (7). As D.19.2.30.3 (cited below) implies, the final *probatio* customarily took place at the end of the term. In a job let out with the *merces* given *in pedes mensurasue*, the approval coincided with a final measurement of the work to determine the cost of the work. This method of payment was more suitable for certain jobs, for example, stone-work, roads and walls. But in either case, the employer was entitled to a final approval. Therefore, the relationship between payment and approval is less significant than it might seem at first glance : approval entitled the builder to payment, but payment by the employer did not necessarily imply his approval. The opinion of Javolenus in D.19.2.51.1 also diminishes the importance of payment in establishing an implied approval (see above at Chapter III, section C).

In addition to the provision for the price of the whole job, the contract could also include *leges* providing for payments to specialized workers employed to complete components of the structure.

> Alfenus, (3 *dig. a Paulo epit.*) D.19.2.30.3
>
> *Qui aedem faciendam locauerat, in lege dixerat : 'quoad in opus lapidis opus erit, pro lapide et manupretio dominus redemptori in pedes singulos septem dabit' : quaesitum est, utrum factum opus an etiam inperfectum metiri oporteret. respondit etiam imperfectum.*

(5) Florentinus, (7 *inst.*) D.19.2.36 :

Opus quod auersione locatum est donec adprobetur, conductoris periculum est : quod uero ita conductum sit, ut in pedes mensurasue praestetur, eatenus conductoris periculo est, quatenus admensum non sit : et in utraque causa nociturum locatori, si per eum steterit, quo minus opus adprobetur uel admetiatur. si tamen ui maiore opus prius interciderit quam adprobaretur, locatoris periculo est, nisi si aliud actum sit : non enim amplius praestari locatori oporteat quam quod sua cura atque opera consecutus esset.

For a discussion of other legal issues raised in this text, see above at Chapter III, section B.

(6) See above all, J. A. C. Thomas, 679.

(7) See also S. Martin, *SZ* 103 (1986) 321-337.

The text probably reflects the opinion of Servius ([8]). The fragment cites the words of a clause specifying payment of 7 sesterces per foot to the contractor for materials and labor required for the stonework in the building. The jurist must decide whether the work should be measured (and approved ?) twice, once before the job is completed and again at the end of the work. Alfenus/Servius responds that the stonework should also be measured while the rest of the job is still in progress, with the result that it will have been measured twice.

The situation underlying the text reveals an interesting feature of the organization of the contract. The job calls for certain types of specialized labor, such as stonework, and the contractor is in charge of procuring the worker and materials and paying him for the work. The contractor's responsibility for the hire of subordinate workers, even those who are outside of his own area of expertise, suggests that his job has a substantial organizational component. Other texts allude to this practice ([9]). In the case under consideration, the stoneworker has finished the required work and would like his pay. The contractor, who had probably only received one half of the total contract price at the beginning of the job, seeks the interim measurement of the stonework in order to obtain the amount owed to the stoneworker.

Thomas asserted that this measurement also implied an approval of the work during the construction, which may have exonerated the contractor

(8) L. DE SARLO, *Alfeno Varo e i suoi Digesti* (1940) 101-102, assumes that the rule must be from Servius. Presumably the content of the opinion is from the late Republic. Paul may have abbreviated the text, see T. MAYER-MALY, *LC* 107. AMIRANTE's assertion, *Bull.* 62 (1959) 73, that Paul inserted *aedem faciendam locauerat,* the *actio locati* not being available for an *opus* before Labeo, has not gained acceptance, see above at Chapter I and C. A. CANNATA, *Colpa* 173-174 ; J. A. C. THOMAS, 673-689 ; M. KASER, *IURA* 11 (1960) 233.

(9) Contractors often hired *fabri* to work on the job, see CIC. 2 *Verr.* i.147 ; VENULEIUS, D.45.1.137.3. These workers were probably hired through *locatio conductio operarum.* The *Basilica* version of this text (20.1.30.3 = HEIMB. 2.355-356, SCHELT. BT 991, BS 1195) supports my interpretation. These sources indicate that *locatio conductio operis* implies a considerable degree of organizational control : the *redemptor* does not have a construction firm in the modern sense, with the capacity to undertake large jobs involving many types of skills or the ability to create 'developments' as is common today. He does, nevertheless, employ several other builders, and procure specialized artisans when needed, so as to be able to complete an entire house or *insula.* The organization of construction of domestic and other small projects has only recently achieved the capacity to evolve beyond the pattern of many small contractors working independently, see E. W. COONEY, *Economic History Review* 8 (1955-56) 167-176 and especially 167-168, on the types of organization found in the construction industry in Victorian England.

from further responsibility for the stonework ([10]). This interpretation derives from Florentinus (D.19.2.36) who states that jobs with a price calculated in units of measure must be measured in order to accomplish approval and release from responsibility. As we have seen, this text provides no explicit evidence for interim approval of individual units of work. In D.19.2.30.3, the jurist grants early measurement as an exception to normal practice solely for the purpose of securing the payment of the price of the stonework. To interpret this measurement as *probatio* confuses the primary function of measurement (ascertaining the final price) with a secondary function accruing to it through usage (simultaneously inspecting the work for faults). If we simply accept the first measurement as a way of reckoning the stoneworker's payment, it is possible to avoid inferring into the law confusing exceptions and limitations upon the employer's right to a final approval of the whole structure, a right this text assumes from the outset ([11]).

Another problem emerges from an examination of this text. If the builder sought to obtain payment by bringing an action during the contract term, would this not extinguish the obligation ? In principle, of course, this would be the result of an action, but the builder could insert a *praescriptio* into the formula and thereby limit the scope of the claim to the amount already due, in this case, the cost of the measured stonework. The action would not jeopardize the existence of the obligation ([12]).

Construction projects often require additional expense above the original contract price, and several sources suggest that this was as commonplace in the Roman world as it is today ([13]). Extra costs result from diverse causes, but actions brought by either party usually sought to recover expenses incurred in correcting defects or restoring damaged work. One text presents an extreme case of cost overrun :

Labeo, (5 *post. a Iau. epit.*) D.19.2.60.4

Mandaui tibi, ut excuteres, quanti uillam aedificare uelles : renuntiasti mihi ducentorum impensam excutere : certa mercede opus tibi locaui, postea comperi

(10) See J. A. C. Thomas, 674-675 and 677-678, where he accepts the analysis of F. M. De Robertis, *I rapporti*, 160. Cf. the *Basilica* text cited note 9.

(11) J. A. C. Thomas, 678, seems undecided and almost willing to concede two approvals.

(12) L. De Sarlo (cited note 8), 101-102, interprets D.19.2.30.3 as allowing an action in the middle of the term through the use of a *praescriptio*. On *praescriptio*, see M. Kaser, *RZ* 192, and Gaius 4.130-133.

(13) See especially Gel. 19.10.2 : *Cumque architectus dixisset necessaria uideri esse sestertia ferme trecenta, unus ex amicis Frontonis : 'et praeterpropter', inquit, 'alia quinquaginta'.* See below at p. 120 and note 20 on Vitr. 10 *praef.* 1-2.

> *non posse minoris trecentorum eam uillam constare : data autem tibi erant centum, ex quibus cum partem impendisses, uetui te opus facere. dixi, si opus facere perseueraueris, ex locato tecum agere, ut pecuniae mihi reliquum restituas.*

The text is not interpolated ([14]). A party interested in having a villa built commissions an estimate from a contractor through mandate ([15]). On the basis of the estimate, the parties conclude a contract through *locatio* with a price of 200. The payment schedule is familiar from other sources : the contractor receives half the *merces* in advance ; presumably the other half was payable after completion and approval.

During construction the builder learns that the project cannot be completed for less than 300, 50% more than the contract price. The reason for the increased expense is not made clear – it is possible that the builder encountered difficulty after beginning the construction, for example, a rise in the cost of materials or hired help. Under the contract as it was formed, the builder probably had hoped to complete the work for less than 200 so that he could earn a profit. The rise in cost means that fulfillment of the contract will result in considerable loss, and the builder has apparently stopped working in the hope that the employer will agree to pay the extra 100. The employer, faced with the prospect of a builder who will not complete the work, refuses to pay the extra costs.

Labeo allows the employer to give the builder notice of his intention to terminate the contract. The text suggests that the employer must make a formal notification of this intent which includes a prohibition against any further attempt to continue the contract by building. No suit results from the employer's decision to terminate the obligation ; the contract ceases to exist, leaving both parties as they were at the moment of recission. The employer adds as a deterrent to any further building the threat of a suit for the *pecuniae reliquum*. This probably means that the builder is not required to restore the 100 (or any unspent portion of it) unless he ignores the prohibition ([16]).

(14) T. Mommsen read *impensam <te> ; tecum <me> agere.* The opinion may be Labeo's, see O. Lenel, *Paling.* I 311, and F. Schulz, *History* 206-209.

(15) In the contract of mandate, a person assumed the duty to perform a service in the interest of the mandator or a third party. The service had to be gratuitous. The *mandatarius* could claim no pay. He could, however, sue for reimbursement of his expenses through the *actio mandati contraria*, see M. Kaser, *RPR*[2] I 577-580.

(16) An alternative interpretation is that he must return the unspent portion and, if he continues, risk a suit for the spent portion. R. Düll, *SZ* 69 (1952) 420-427, assumes that the employer has the right to claim the unspent portion of the advance.

Although the text makes no mention of the employer's plans, he is presumably free to contract with another builder for the completion of the job if he so chooses.

Labeo's decision to allow the termination of the contract is fairly drastic. He doesn't compel the employer to wait to seek a remedy until the contract term has elapsed. Instead, he allows the employer to interpret the builder's actions as evidence of his repudiation of the contract. This comes quite close to the modern concept of anticipatory breach of contract ([17]). This solution was doubtless beneficial to both parties. The builder is released from his responsibility to complete the work and avoids the consequences of an action based upon his failure to perform. The employer loses his 100, but some of this may be recuperable in the value of the work already done. He is free to find another builder without the delay involved in waiting until the end of the term.

A passage from Cicero's correspondance with his brother provides an interesting parallel ([18]). Quintus' *uilicus,* Nicephorus, has given an estimate and contracted to build a small structure on the property at Laterium. When Quintus began to increase the amount of work without renegotiating the price, Nicephorus withdrew from the contract. As in D.19.2.60.4, the fundamental assumptions upon which the agreement was based have been altered unilaterally, and the other party withdraws from the contract.

Labeo was certainly influenced by the size of the extra expense demanded by the builder : the degree of difference between the original price and the newly discovered cost is great. A small overrun, for example, 10% or even 25%, was probably anticipated, and normal practice in construction may have conditioned the employer to expect modest extra expenses ([19]). Of course, the employer would have to agree to pay anything over the contract price, and in this case, the amount of the overrun, 50%, prompted the employer to

(17) On anticipatory breach of contract, see 11 WILLISTON, *Contracts* 1324 (3rd ed. 1957).

(18) CIC. *Q.fr.* 3.1.5 :

> *Nicephorum, uilicum tuum, sane probaui quaesiuique ex eo, ecquid ei de illa aedificatiuncula Lateri, de qua mecum locutus es, mandauisses. tum is mihi respondit, se ipsum eius operis HS $\overline{XVI}$ conductorem fuisse, sed te postea multa addidisse ad opus, nihil ad pretium ; itaque id se omisisse.*

Most scholars have assumed that Nicephorus, as a *uilicus,* was a slave, see H. KAUFMANN, 211-212 ; K. D. WHITE, *Roman Farming* (1970) 350-354, and cf. R. BEARE, *CQ* 28 (1978) 398-401. See above at Chapter II, note 53.

(19) See GEL. 19.10.2, cited above at note 13. When builders quote a price of 300,000 to Fronto for the construction of a bath, a friend interjects that he must assume that an extra 50,000, one sixth of the price, will be required.

rethink his obligation. The Roman practice in defining an acceptable cost overrun may have a parallel in the Ephesian law to which Vitruvius refers in the preface to his tenth book ([20]). In Ephesus, according to Vitruvius, an architect furnishes to the city an estimate of the cost of a job and must register personal property as security. If the project is completed for the exact contract cost, the architect is honored with a decree. If the cost exceeds the contract price up to 25%, the state pays this amount. However, if the cost exceeds 25%, the additional completion costs are taken from the architect's property. Vitruvius goes on to lament the lack of any such practice at Rome in spite of the great need for a control upon the spending habits of unscrupulous architects. Although the practice he describes is not found in Rome in the administration of public construction, Vitruvius may have been voicing a common concern in his call for 'acceptable limits' to increases in building costs ([21]). Some similar rule of thumb may have operated in the private building industry and guided the employer in determining how much extra he might be required to pay when a building project had exceeded the original price.

(20) VITR. 10 *praef.* 1-2. R. DÜLL (cited note 16), 420-427, argues that the practice in private law reflected in D.19.2.60.4 was influenced by this law, but already existed in public law in the use of *praedes.* There is no evidence that this was the case. On the use of sureties in public and private contracts, see below Chapter III, section E.

(21) On the Greek practice in organizing public works, see J. J. COULTON, *Ancient Greek Architects at Work* (1977) 15-29, and A. BURFORD, *The Greek Temple Builders at Epidauros* (1969) 98 and 164-166. The architect designed the building and estimated the costs ; he was also responsible if the contractor exceeded them, even though his participation in the building was only supervisory. The evidence for the activities of Roman architects is uninstructive on this point, but Düll's assumption that *redemptor* and architect are the same person is not to be accepted.

SECTION E

DAMAGES AND PENALTIES AVAILABLE ON A CONSTRUCTION CONTRACT AND PROVISIONS FOR SECURING THE CONTRACT

When either party brought an action on the contract, he extinguished the obligation and attempted to recover a sum which would recompense him for loss resulting from the actions of the other party (1). Our knowledge of the methods used for the calculation of remedies is rather restricted owing to the silence of the legal sources concerning this aspect of the trial ; much of the relevant discussion may have been excised by the compilers. There was no generalized theory of damages based upon such considerations as "putting the party in the condition he would have been if had the contract been performed" (2). The actual calculation of a monetary award was evidently somewhat flexible, and the *iudex* decided the amount of the final judgment according to practices developed in individual areas of law according to general guidelines set by the jurists.

Although the texts furnish little explicit information concerning the types of damages available through an action on a construction contract, a comparison of the sources indicates that certain patterns developed in calculating and providing for fixed damage assessments. The actual remedies available through the *actio locati* or *conducti* remain obscure, but seem to involve the builder's right to the *merces* versus the employer's interest in obtaining either the completed structure or the completion costs. In addition to the contractual remedy, the employer could also provide for further payments by supplementing the contract with stipulations for specific damages or penalties payable if the builder exceeded the time limit set for the work. Construction contracts in both *locatio* and *stipulatio* were also guar-

(1) On other ways for the contract to come to an end, see Chapter III, section D, on the termination of the contract because of cost overrun. The builder can also extinguish the obligation by performing, so long as the employer has not brought an action.

(2) On modern theories of damages, see P. ATIYAH, *An Introduction to the Law of Contract*[3] (1981) 303-323 ; L. FRIEDMAN, *Contract Law in America* (1965) 124-129, describes the development of fixed damage estimates in construction contracts in the nineteenth century. On the more fluid Roman notion, see D. MEDICUS, *Id quod interest* (1962) 1-3, and H. HONSELL, *Quod interest in bonae fidei iudicium* (1969) 1-2, who disagree as to the method of evaluation implied by *id quod interest*, cf. D. MEDICUS in his review of Honsell, *SZ* 88 (1971) 446-453.

anteed by sureties who promised to meet the financial obligations of the builder if he were unable to do so. The contracts were then formed as 'packages', and through the ancillary stipulations the parties anticipated and protected themselves against some of the insecurity inherent in construction contracts.

I. – Remedies Available through the Actions on the Contracts

In *locatio conductio*, an action brought by either party involved three main areas of dispute for which some remedy would be available : destruction arising during the contract term, *improbatio* and the builder's delay or default. In each instance, the damaged party would have to decide whether or not to bring an action based upon his perceived chances of success. The jurists' law would provide guidelines for making this decision.

Once the formula for an action was obtained by either party, the contract was extinguished. From that point forward, the activity of the contract was to be estimated in terms of a monetary award, the *condemnatio pecuniaria*. Since the action on an obligation to construct a building is not for a fixed sum but involves the value of a job of work, Medicus expected to find the use of the expression *id quod interest* in discussions of the damages available through the *actio locati-conducti* (3). This method of calculating damages, which is based roughly on an estimation of the plaintiff's 'interest' in the defendant's failure to perform, would allow a flexible calculation of the employer's loss if, for example, the builder failed to complete the job. But there is no indication that the *actio locati* or *conducti* gave rise to estimates of the plaintiff's 'interest' damages. The only fixed sum available is the *merces*, the amount owed to the builder at the end of the job, which presumably functioned as the point of departure in discussions of the monetary award resulting from a successful action. Of course the *merces* represented the original estimation of the value of the contract and would not necessarily be equivalent to the expenses incurred by either party if the cost of the completed structure had increased as a result of the builder's activities or other damaging events. This may explain the common use of ancillary stipulations for damages.

When the building suffered harm during the contract term as a result of natural causes or inherent defects in the building site, the jurists concern themselves with deciding who must bear the risk for loss (*periculum*) and

(3) D. Medicus (cited note 2), 185.

give no indication of how this loss was to be reckoned. The employer is reluctant to pay *merces* for a building which has been destroyed either in part or totally and would try to obtain repairs without having to pay more than he had originally planned. The builder has seen his work destroyed by forces which may have been beyond his control. He would like to discharge his obligation somehow and collect the *merces*, if not in full, at least a *pro rata* share. According to Paul in D.19.2.62, the builder bore the *periculum* for faults in the work, and presumably this means he had no claim to *merces* if the destruction resulted from his *uitium* in carrying out the job. If he tried to rebuild the structure in order to be released from his obligation, he did so at his own expense (4). If, however, the destruction emanated from the building site, the employer was responsible for paying the *merces* and also for completion costs if the builder was to finish the work.

When the employer found faults in the builder's work during *probatio*, he probably refused to pay the remaining *merces* until the corrections had been done. In public law, the contractor was required to repair the faults or to pay for a new contract (5). It seems likely that many minor disputes over quality or specifications were settled long before the parties considered bringing an action, with the builder simply redoing the work at his own expense. However, the case underlying D.19.2.60.3 was probably typical of private law actions brought for *improbatio* (6). The builder incorporated some changes into a structure at the request of the employer, who then dies. The heir, who was not aware of the changes, brought an action on the grounds that the work did not conform to specifications. Had the action been successful, the builder would have been responsible for an estimate of the cost of the changes, and perhaps this was deducted from the *merces* he was to receive. As in the cases on risk, the remedy seems to approximate the final cost of the building which has increased owing to various circumstances arising during the work.

The loss or damage suffered by the employer when the builder delays or defaults include both the cost of completing the work and extra expenses arising from his inability to dispose of the structure as he had planned, whether for commercial exploitation or for his own habitation. The loss resulting from delay was not easily reckoned in terms of the *merces*. The contractual remedy, which is unattested, may have denied the worker some portion of his *merces* in relationship to the amount of building yet to be

(4) On this text, see above Chapter III, section B. J. A. C. Thomas, 682, assumes that *periculum conductoris* means 'no *opus*, no pay'.
(5) Cic. 2 *Verr.* i 130-150.
(6) On *probatio* and D.19.2.60.3, see above at Chapter III, section C.

done ([7]). The employer could, however, protect himself in advance against the contractor's delay by including a clause allowing a new contract to be formed immediately after the *dies operis* had arrived :

Ulpian, (32 *ad ed.*) D.19.2.13.10

Si lege operis locandi comprehensum esset, ut, si ad diem effectum non esset, relocare id liceret, non alias prior conductor ex locato tenebitur, quam si eadem lege relocatum esset : nec ante relocari id potest, quam dies efficiendi praeterisset.

The text is probably sound ([8]). The parties have appended to the contract a clause (*lex*) which permits, but does not require, the employer to let out the contract to another builder if the first builder has not finished the work on time. The contract names a completion date. Ulpian's interpretation of the clause implies that the employer has exercised his option by concluding a contract with a second builder. He now seeks to bring an *actio locati* against the first builder.

Ulpian will allow the action only if the project has been contracted to the second builder under the terms of the *lex locationis* described at the beginning of the text. Therefore, the employer had to meet two conditions in order to replace the builder : the work must be incomplete ; the contract term must have elapsed. He concludes by saying that the employer cannot hire a second builder before the completion date has passed ([9]).

This final sentence gives us a clue to the factual situation behind the decision. The employer anticipates that the first builder cannot complete the work on time and seeks to hire another builder under the clause before the *dies operis* ([10]). The jurist is unwilling to allow the employer to terminate the contract unilaterally by bringing an action based on delay before the completion date has passed. This resistance is characteristic of the juristic attitude

(7) This may explain the use of ancillary stipulations, see D.19.2.58.1 above at Chapter III, section A, and below at section II.

(8) T. MAYER-MALY, *LC* 218-219, brackets out the last phrase, *nec-praeterisset* (see further on his criticisms below at note 9).

(9) T. MAYER-MALY, *LC* 219, argues on the basis of the scholia to the *Basilica* text 20.1.13.10 (= HEIMB. 2.340, SCHELT. BT 985 and BS 1178) that the second contract cannot be made unless it contains the same clause as the first contract specifying a time limit. According to this analysis, the second builder must be held to the same term as an implicit gauge of its fairness. (If the first builder had completed even 50% of the job, this clause would be meaningless.) However, the phrase *eadem lege* need not describe the content of the new agreement, but rather how the new contract must be undertaken : "under the terms of the same clause".

(10) The scholiasts on the *Basilica* text (cited previous note) are unanimous in adopting this interpretation.

towards early lawsuits in construction contracts (see above at Chapter III, section A), and underlying this attitude are two lines of thought. First, the jurists tend to preserve agreements as the parties have framed them, so, in this instance, the employer cannot unilaterally reinterpret the clause he had included for his own protection ([11]). Second, there is a tendency not to allow anticipatory breach of contract ([12]). This is also apparent in the law on stipulations for construction. If the employer hired a second builder prematurely, he would lose his *actio locati*, and the first contractor would be released from liability for delay.

No mention is made in the text of the remedy sought by the employer, but the clause providing for another contract strongly suggests that the builder was responsible for completion costs and, more specifically, the price of the new contract. This inference is supported by the factual circumstances in D.46.1.44 (see below at section III), in which sureties are taken for the amount of a new contract for completion. The typical procedure was to bring an action against the sureties or the builder for the price of the new contract as the award. But this could only be successful if the employer first allowed the entire contract period to elapse ([13]).

As this brief overview has shown, the causes for actions involve an increase in the cost of completion, either because corrections have to be made or damaging events have occurred. The extra costs would be subject to dispute either explicitly or implicitly. In a typical contract, the builder had received half of the *merces* at the beginning of construction, which was certainly quickly spent on materials, labor and equipment. Subsequent claims by the employer involving assessments for amounts greater than the remaining portion of the *merces* to be paid would require the builder to furnish more from his own resources. For example, in D.19.2.13.10, the builder would presumably be liable for the cost of the new contract. Often the sureties would guarantee payment of the damages. In general, the employer's claim would be to avoid payment of the *merces* still owing and to recapture a portion of the *merces* already spent so as to be able to finish the job. There is no way to determine whether the builder's liability on the contract was limited to the *merces*.

In contracts concluded through *stipulatio*, the condemnation available through the action was for *id quod interest*. If the stipulator was able to

(11) This rule is discussed in Chapter III, section A.

(12) See H. BENÖHR, *Das sogenannte Synallagma in den Konsensualkontrakten* (1965) 98-108.

(13) A complete analysis of D.46.1.44 is given below in section III.

establish that the builder had not performed, he was able to collect a sum which corresponded in some measure to his losses resulting from the builder's failure to complete the job ([14]). This was a common technique for obligations for something other than a fixed sum. Since the contract was unilateral, the action involved the employer's claim for the work ([15]). Claims on stipulations were mostly framed in terms of timely completion of the work, regardless of the reason for the delay. The consequences of this are well illustrated in D.45.1.15. The structure has been damaged or destroyed by fire and the builder is required to rebuild at his own expense. The jurist grants him the entire contract period anew for the work ([16]). If the builder completes the structure within the new term, he will incur no damages for delay, but must meet his obligation in spite of the large expense involved in rebuilding.

II. – Ancillary Clauses and Stipulations

In addition to the remedy available through an action on the contract, the employer could provide for the payment of various types of damage assessments by adding to the agreement a conditional stipulation whereby the builder agrees to pay a specific amount if he fails to complete the work on time. Three sources provide evidence for these additional stipulations : a fixed penalty (D.45.1.113 pr.) ; payment of *quanti ea res erit* (D.45.1.72.1) ; payment of *id quod interest* (D.19.2.58.1). The stipulations usually fall due if the work has not been completed by a certain date (D.45.1.113 pr. ; 45.1.72.1). In one case, the condition is expressed without a date (D.19.2.58.1).

This procedure was attractive because the amount of compensation was assured provided that the employer could prove his case. The award, whether specified in a lump sum or in a more flexible formulation, would be more substantial than that obtainable through the *actio locati.* Since the stipulations provide for payments incurred by the builder's delay, the proof is relatively simple. The texts presented in this section and the following section on sureties imply that construction contracts in *locatio conductio* were typically formulated to include the principal agreement accompanied by stipulations for extra penalties and provisions for sureties to guarantee the payment of the

(14) At least according to D. Medicus (cited note 2), 212-217.

(15) The builder's claim for payment is completely unattested, and we do not even know for certain how the parties provided for the reciprocal obligation to pay for the work, see Chapter I.

(16) On D.45.1.15, see above Chapter III, section B.

damage awards. Construction contracts in *stipulatio* did not require the mechanism of ancillary stipulations, but could be accompanied by penalty clauses and arrangements for sureties.

Stipulations for the payment of a penalty were a common method of assuring the creditor compensation if the contractor defaulted. Penalty clauses were often concluded separately through a stipulation to guarantee a primary obligation ([17]). Usually, when the penalty was incurred by delay, both the action on the stipulation and that on the primary obligation ran concurrently. A stipulation for a penalty bound the builder to pay a fixed sum if the work was not complete by a certain date, and the employer may have chosen to use this type of clause specifically to deter the builder from delaying. The goal of such clauses was not to offer a compensation for any loss suffered as a result of the builder's default. The idea was rather to extract a penalty, and so employers would use these clauses when timely performance was especially important.

Proculus discusses a dispute over a penalty stipulation :

> Proculus, (2 *epist.*) D.45.1.113 pr.
>
> *Cum stipulatus sim mihi, Procule, si opus arbitratu meo ante kalendas Iunias effectum non sit, poenam, et protuli diem : putasne uere me posse dicere arbitratu meo opus effectum non esse ante kalendas Iunias, cum ipse arbitrio meo aliam diem operi laxiorem dederim ? Proculus respondit : non sine causa distinguendum est interesse, utrum per promissorem mora non fuisset, quo minus opus ante kalendas Iunias ita, uti stipulatione comprehensum erat, perficeretur, an, cum iam opus effici non posset ante kalendas Iunias, stipulator diem in kalendis Augustis protulisset. Nam si tum diem stipulator protulit, cum iam opus ante kalendas Iunias effici non poterat, puto poenam esse commissam nec ad rem pertinere, quod aliquod tempus ante kalendas Iunias fuit, quo stipulator non desiderauit id ante kalendas Iunias effici, id est quo non est arbitratus ut fieret quod fieri non poterat. Aut si hoc falsum est, etiam si stipulator pridie kalendas Iunias mortuus esset, poena commissa non esset, quoniam mortuus arbitrari non potuisset et aliquod tempus post mortem eius operi perficiendo superfuisset. et propemodum etiam si ante kalendas Iunias futurum esse coepit opus ante eam diem effici non posse, poena commissa est.*

Much of this difficult text has been considered interpolated. However, apart from the apparent gloss (*in kalendis Augustis*), the text is probably sound ([18]). The fragment is in question-and-answer form. The parties have

(17) In general on penalty clauses, see R. KNÜTEL, *SP* 10-17 and 25-33, on penalty clauses as an indirect means of persuasion.

(18) The most thorough discussion of this text is in R. KNÜTEL, *SP* 103-106, with

stipulated that if a job has not been completed by the kalends of June, the promissor will pay a penalty to the stipulator. Before this term has expired, the stipulator extended the completion date for the job. He asks whether or not he can claim the penalty, even though he has extended the time limit on the primary obligation. Proculus does not specifically mention the contract to which the penalty clause is appended. Yet the language used to express the content of the obligation is consistent with that commonly used in construction (*opus efficere*). It seems likely that the principal obligation was one for construction either in *locatio* or *stipulatio* ([19]).

Proculus' response is complex and somewhat strident. He begins by attempting to distinguish two categories of delay. The first type is delay that is not the fault of the promissor. The second is delay that was recognized before the end of the contract term and resulted in a time extension. The bulk of Proculus' response applies to the second case. The point of the distinction is not clearly expressed, but is crucial in deciding whether or not the penalty will be incurred. The stipulator cannot invoke the penalty clause if the delay was not the fault of the builder. The second alternative furnishes the antithesis, although obliquely : the delay was the builder's fault, and it was detected well before the completion date. This caused the stipulator to extend the *dies.* The builder argues that the penalty has not been incurred on the grounds that the extension implicitly applied to the penalty clause. Proculus does not agree : under these circumstances, the builder must pay the penalty.

Proculus' assertion apparently contradicted the prevailing opinion. The wording of the response (*puto-pertinere*) seems directed at specific objections. Proculus maintained that the penalty was incurred before the completion date when the stipulator recognized the builder's delay and extended the contract term. The proponents of the alternative view may have required a formal, negative *arbitratus* on June first in order for the penalty to fall due ([20]). Proculus dismisses this as unnecessary : the stipulator had recognized that the builder could not possibly finish the job ; why require a further verification of this fact ?

bibliography. He defends the classicity of the fragment. See also M. TALAMANCA, *Ricerche in tema di compromissum* (1958) 59 n. 52 ; C. KRAMPE, *Proculi Epistulae* (1970) 62 ff. ; K. VISKY, *St. Volterra I* (1971) 597-635 ; P. VOCI, *St. Volterra* III (1971) 350-351.

(19) So too C. A. CANNATA, *Colpa* 178-179, who believes that the primary obligation in this passage must have been a contract for construction in *locatio conductio.* In general on this text, see R. KNÜTEL, *SP* 31 and 103. It seems unlikely, as he points out, that the content of the *Epistulae* was theoretical, but see C. KRAMPE (cited note 18).

(20) So R. KNÜTEL, *SP* 105.

In support of his own opinion, Proculus relies upon a *reductio ad absurdum* to demonstrate the inherent inferiority of the opposing view. Proculus maintains that the penalty is incurred even before the fixed date. It makes no difference that between the time extension and the kalends of June there was a space of time in which the stipulator was to make an evaluation (*arbitratus*) of the work and decide that it could not be completed. The extension makes this *arbitratus* superfluous. The consequences of rejecting this analysis would be that a penalty could not be incurred if the stipulator died the day before the kalends of June, even if there was no hope of the work being finished on time : the dead man would not be able to perform the required evaluation.

Proculus diverged from the prevailing view presumably because of the exceptional factual circumstances of the case. The stipulator has already agreed to postpone the action on the principal obligation, probably at the request of the builder, who is evidently responsible for the delay. The employer is willing to allow the builder to discharge his obligation, but this does not imply a tacit extension of the deadline on the penalty clause. As Knütel points out, *propemodum* has a limiting force upon the last statement which is not intended to become a general maxim ([21]). It is unlikely that Proculus would be willing to extend the rule here to apply to other cases of delay, for example, to allow in every case the early decision that a penalty is due when delay begins to become apparent ([22]). He is preserving the intent of the employer in fixing the penalty clause, while allowing the parties to renegotiate the term of the principal obligation.

Stipulations for payment of *id quod interest* or *quanti ea res erit* by a defaulting builder offered the employer another way to hold the builder financially responsible for the consequences of delay ([23]). In D.19.2.58.1,

(21) R. KNÜTEL, *SP* 104-106, with earlier bibliography.

(22) See Proculus in Paul, (2 *ad Sab.*) D.45.1.8 :

> *In illa stipulatione : 'si kalendis Stichum non dederis, decem dare spondes ?' mortuo homine quaeritur, an statim ante kalendas agi possit. Sabinus Proculus exspectandum diem actori putant, quod est uerius : tota enim obligatio sub condicione et in diem collata est et licet ad condicionem committi uideatur, dies tamen superest. sed cum eo, qui ita promisit : 'si intra kalendas digito caelum non tetigerit', agi protinus potest. haec et Marcellus probat.*

This text is of special interest since Proculus is upholding the letter of the stipulation and enforcing an action on the fixed *dies.* This demonstrates the exceptional nature of the rule in D.45.1.113 pr. which depends upon a specific set of circumstances. Not the least of these is that the parties have agreed upon the change in terms while the obligation is still running.

(23) See D. MEDICUS (cited note 2), 185-186 and 44-45. The procedure whereby the employer would bring his action either on one suit or the other is not specified. Perhaps he

Labeo refers to a stipulation providing for the builder's payment of *id quod interest* to the *locator* if the work is not done. A judgment for *id quod interest* would involve an evaluation by the *iudex* of the money value of the employer's 'interest' in the builder's default. There is no single method for reckoning this amount, and it probably could include compensation for losses incurred as a consequence of the builder's default. The calculation was presumably conducted according to guidelines which developed in specific areas of law.

Ulpian, in D.45.1.72.1, mentions a stipulation for another type of payment :

> Ulpian, (20 *ad ed.*) D.45.1.72.1
>
> *Si quis ita stipulatus sit : 'si ante kalendas Martias primas opus perfectum non erit, tum quanti id opus erit, tantam pecuniam dari ?', diem promissionis cedere non ex quo locatum est opus, sed post kalendas Martias, quia nec conueniri ante kalendas Martias reus promittendi poterat.*

The text is not interpolated ([24]). The employer has concluded a stipulation binding the promissor to pay *quanti ea res erit* if a job is not complete before the kalends of March. The jurist, asked when the action might be brought for the payment of this sum, gives his opinion that the promise falls due after the kalends of March ([25]).

Quanti ea res erit was a method of calculating the value of the object of an action and was applied to obligations involving a *certum* or fixed sum. If the object was not specifically a *certum*, by the high classical period the jurists were evaluating damages in *quanti ea res erit* to include what the injured party had suffered. The judgment, therefore, could range from an approximation of the value of the object to an amount similar to that for *id quod interest* ([26]).

was allowed to chose whether he preferred to sue on the primary obligation or the stipulation. In cases of delay, he would probably prefer to try the action on the stipulation first and may have been allowed in certain cases also to bring the *actio locati.* On concurrence problems in general when ancillary clauses are appended, see R. KNÜTEL, *SP* 262-290 and 320-334 on Julian, (3 *ad Vrseium Ferocem*) D.19.2.28. On the different views as to how *id quod interest* was calculated, see above at note 2.

(24) The text has not been considered seriously interpolated. G. BESELER, *TR* 10 (1930) 231, makes a few minor alterations to connect this passage more explicitly with the *Lex Furia.*

(25) This opinion is typical of those on *stipulationes* for an obligation whose fulfillment requires time, see above at Chapter III, section A.

(26) On the calculation of *quanti ea res erit,* see M. KASER, *RZ* 242-243 and *Quanti ea res est* (1935) 165 ; 206 ff. See also K. BELOW, *Die Haftung für 'lucrum cessans' im römischen Recht* (1964) 77 ff.

III. – Securing the Contract

The practice of requiring that the builder furnish sureties was well established in construction law in the Republic. The employer's goal was to seek protection against the potential expense to be incurred if the builder either failed to complete his work or did a faulty job. Sureties also guaranteed that the builder's insolvency would not prevent the recovery of damages.

The use of sureties in public law is outlined in several sources ([27]). Generally, the magistrate in charge of letting the contract determined how many sureties (*praedes*) were necessary and how much property had to be registered as security. The *lex parieti faciundo Puteolana* records five names, the first followed by *idem praes* and a sum of money ([28]). The sureties are pledged for 1,500 sesterces, presumably the amount of the *merces.* The designation *idem praes* is puzzling but may indicate that C. Blossius is both contractor and surety ([29]). This conjecture seems valid particularly since no other contractor is named. The *praedia* pledged by Blossius would insure the contractor's ability to pay in case of difficulties. The other names may have been those of *praedes* who agreed orally to be responsible for the same obligation as the principal, as in private contracts, but who were not required to register property ([30]).

The sureties were released from responsibility along with the builder after *probatio* ([31]). If he did not adequately execute the work, the magistrates could sell the *praedia* in order to pay for corrections ([32]). Alternatively, the *praedes*

(27) *Lex Municipii Malacitani, FIRA* I # 24 = *ILS* 6089 c. 60 ; 63-65 ; see also, Cic. 2 *Verr.* i 130-150 (see further below) ; Polybius 6.17 ; *FIRA* I # 18. For the *lex Puteolana,* see below at note 28. See E. Badian, *Publicans and Sinners* (1972) 68-69. Earlier comprehensive works are P. Viard, *Le Praes* (1907), F. Kniep, *Societas publicanorum* (1896) especially at 340, and M. Kaser, *Das altrömische Ius* (1949) 272-273.

(28) *FIRA* III # 153 = *ILLRP* 518 : *C. Blossius Q.f. (sestertiis) MD idem praes. : Q. Fuficius Q.f., Cn. Tetteius Q.f., C. Granius C.f., Ti. Crassicius.* On this, see T. Wiegand, 688-693. On the word *praes,* in addition to the works cited above, see also, Var. *L.* 6.74.

(29) T. Wiegand, 690-691, accepts Mommsen's interpretation that Blossius was both *redemptor* and *praes.* See also E. Badian (cited note 27), 68 ; J. L. D. Pearse, 13 ; E. Kaden, *Études sur l'origine du contrat d'entreprise dans le droit romain* in *Rec. trav. Fac. Droit Genève* (1938) 204-207. These men seem to be local citizens and property owners. On the Blossii in southern Italy and Puteoli, see J. H. D'Arms, *AJA* 77 (1973) 161-162.

(30) So E. Badian (cited note 27), 68-69.

(31) This is implied in the *lex parieti faciundo Puteolana* (see above at note 28). See R. Samter, *SZ* 26 (1905) 142, and T. Wiegand, 684-685.

(32) The process is described in the *lex Municipii Malacitani, FIRA* I # 24 = *ILS* 6089 c. 64-65. See the commentary of E. G. Hardy, *Roman Laws and Charters* (1912, repr. 1977) 77-82.

had to furnish the amount of money judged necessary by the magistrate. One version of this procedure comes from Cicero's account of Verres' administration of the maintenance of the Temple of Castor and Pollux ([33]).

Once Verres had decided to extract from the estate of the minor son of P. Iunius the cost of needless repairs to the *aedes Castoris,* his first step was to declare the temple faulty in a *probatio* (133-134). Then he let a new contract to straighten the columns which were, according to Verres, not sufficiently perpendicular (133 ; 140-141). The second contract, according to Cicero, should have cost very little ; moreover, the *tutores* acting in behalf of the boy Junius would, under normal circumstances, have had the chance to correct the work themselves (141-142). Verres chose to bypass the customary procedure and awarded the contract for an enormous sum to Habonius, one of Junius' tutors, but also Verres' accomplice ([34]). It becomes clear in the account that the person who has pledged his land to secure the original contract is D. Brutus (cos. 77 B.C.) ([35]). In fact, when the second maintenance contract was awarded, he furnished 560,000 sesterces in cash (150). Later, some of this money was returned to him presumably after the boy's estate had made payments. Brutus himself remains very much in the background.

Part of the interest of the episode is that it demonstrates how many individuals were involved in a maintenance contract. The *redemptor,* P. Iunius, described by Cicero as *homo de plebe Romano* (151), is presumably a client of D. Brutus and has provided his son with *tutores* or protectors of equestrian and senatorial rank ([36]). He is a relatively modest individual and evidently required backing and alliances of this magnitude to obtain a state

(33) Cic. 2 *Verr.* i 144 and 150. References to specific chapters are incorporated into the text.

(34) This man, either Habonius or Rabonius, is otherwise unknown. On his name, see C. Nicolet, *L'Ordre équestre à l'époque républicaine* I (1966) 342. He had already arranged with the other guardians to take over the maintenance contract after the death of Iunius (132-134).

(35) On Brutus, see B. C. Bondurant, *Decimus Junius Brutus Albinus* (diss. University of Chicago, 1907) 20-21 ; F. Cowles, *Gaius Verres* (1917) 21-25 ; E. Costa, *La Pretura di Verre* (1907) 7-11.

(36) On Iunius, F. Münzer, *RE* s.v. Iunius # 28 col. 965 (1917), supposes that Iunius is a client of Brutus. C. Nicolet (cited note 34), 341, feels sure that he is a knight. Cicero's description of him implies that he is a member of the subequestrian population. The wife of the elder Iunius subsequently married G. Mustius, described as the boy's stepfather, who was a knight (135 ; 137), F. Münzer, *RE* s.v. Mustius # 2 col. 911 (1935). The other guardians who are mentioned are P. Titius and M. Marcellus (135 ; 153), who is perhaps to be identified with M. Claudius Marcellus, curule aedile in 91, F. Münzer, *RE* s.v. Claudius # 227 col. 2760 (1899). He is described as a *uirum primarium, summo officio ac uirtute praeditum.*

contract. The boy's tutors carry out the actual negotiations with Verres and they are representative of the *publicani* with whom we might expect P. Iunius to be associated ([37]).

In private contracts, the parties regularly enrolled sureties, and the builder's ability to obtain contracts probably depended upon his capacity to secure the agreement. There is no evidence for the Republican practice, but in the Empire the employer usually secured the contract through *fideiussio* ([38]). This arrangement created personal security and consisted of a *stipulatio* to assume the same obligation as the principal debtor ([39]). Building contracts in *locatio* and in *stipulatio* were secured in this way (D.46.1.44 and D.46.3.31). The *fideiussor* assumed all or a portion of the principal debt, but not a greater obligation. The general practice was to obtain several *fideiussores.*

The two texts which record legal problems involving sureties to a construction contract are particularly revealing in that they testify to moments when things have gone wrong. The builder has not fulfilled his obligation, and the employer is attempting to recover the cost of completing the work. In general, the employer brought the action against the sureties or against them jointly with the builder (see D.46.1.44 ; D.46.3.31 and D.45.1.14). In either case, the possibility of another suit on the same basis is extinguished. The payment of the completion costs becomes their burden. Later, if the builder had not paid the sureties, they could proceed against him for reimbursement ([40]).

In D.46.1.44, the *fideiussores* have agreed to guarantee payment of the completion costs if a construction job let under a contract of *locatio conductio* has not been finished by the date specified in the primary contract and in the stipulation binding the *fideiussores.*

> Javolenus, (11 *epist.*) D.46.1.44
>
> *Stipulatus es opus arbitratu tuo ante certam diem fieri, quod si effectum non esset, quanti ut efficiatur opus locasses, tanti fideiussores cepisti : et quia opus effectum non erat, alii locasti et, cum posterior conductor satis non daret, ipse opus fecisti : quaero, an fideiussor teneatur. respondit : secundum ea uerba stipulationis, quae a te proposita sunt, fideiussores non tenentur. non enim id*

(37) See Cic. 2 *Verr.* i 128, an earlier episode involving the knights Cn. Fannius and Q. Tadius who are also involved with contracting.

(38) In general on *fideiussio,* see M. Kaser, *RPR*^{2} I 660-666 ; T. Mayer-Maly, *LC* 99-101.

(39) Gaius 3.116.

(40) M. Kaser, *RPR*^{2} I 665-666.

> *fecisti, quod in stipulatione conuenerat, id est opus alii non locasti, tametsi postea locasti : ea enim locatio, quam secutus <non> es, perinde est, ac si interposita non esset et si statim tu opus facere coepisses.*

The text is sound ([41]). The failure of the first builder to finish the job sets into motion a response which may have been standard in *locatio* as we have already seen in D.19.2.13.10 : the employer seeks a new contract with another builder who will complete the work. He is, however, unable to conclude a second contract because the new builder fails to provide sureties. As a result, the employer finishes the job on his own, probably by hiring available day labor. He then attempts to recover his completion costs by suing the *fideiussores.*

Javolenus releases the sureties from liability, relying upon a strict interpretation of the words of the first stipulation : according to the promise, the sureties were responsible for the price of a second *locatio* for the completion of the work if the first contractor failed to perform on time. As Javolenus interprets the employer's activities, his efforts to comply with the *stipulatio* are not adequate. The fact that there was no second *locatio* concluded to finish the work becomes the only relevant consideration. The jurist refuses to take into account the employer's intention to form a new contract.

The result of this decision may seem unjust. The employer made an attempt to find another builder but, because he was unable to do this, he received none of the completion costs for which he had provided. However, Javolenus was not attempting to deny the employer his remedy. His motivation in interpreting the contract strictly was to hold the employer to the words of his own agreement. The employer had formulated the content of the stipulation for damages so that compensation would equal the price of a new contract. He then failed to follow the plan he had envisioned. If Javolenus allowed the *fideiussores* to be liable, what amount would they pay ? The employer obviously would request a sum equal to his own costs. This amount may have approximated the price of a second contract. Yet Javolenus clearly wants to avoid interfering in the agreement between the parties ; the employer is asking that the law rectify his situation in spite of the fact that he has not quite followed his own provisions. Javolenus resists the employer's request to reformulate the basis of the sureties' obligation.

(41) C. APPLETON, *NRH* 40 (1916) 50, following Mommsen, accepts the reading of the *deteriores* : *secutus <non> es.* So too T. MAYER-MALY, *LC* 100. C. A. CANNATA, *Colpa* 184-186, excises *non enim postea locasti* on the grounds that it is a disconnected gloss and contradictory to the facts of the case. However, since he accepts Appleton's reading, this emendation seems unnecessary.

The second text addresses the sureties' duties from a different point of view ; in case of the builder's default, can the sureties actually complete the job on their own in lieu of paying completion costs ?

> Ulpian, (7 *disp.*) D.46.3.31
>
> *Inter artifices longa differentia est et ingenii et naturae et doctrinae et institutionis. ideo si nauem a se fabricandam quis promiserit uel insulam aedificandam fossamue faciendam 'et hoc specialiter actum est, ut suis operis id perficiat', fideiussor ipse aedificans uel fossam fodiens non consentiente stipulatore non liberabit reum. quare etiam si illis stipulationibus fideiussor accesserit : 'per te non fieri, quo minus mihi ire agere liceat ?', prohibens ire fideiussor stipulationem non committit et, si patientiam praestet, non efficiet, quo minus committatur stipulatio.*

Only the first portion of the text is relevant (*Inter-liberabit reum*) ([42]). Underlying this case there is a contract of stipulation for construction work. An ancillary stipulation binds sureties to be responsible to the employer in case the builder fails to complete the work.

Ulpian's comments reveal some difficulties inherent in binding a person to be equally responsible for an obligation *facere* ([43]). In this case, the *fideiussor* himself wishes to complete the work and thereby release himself and the principal debtor from the obligation and avoid paying damages. Ulpian begins the text with a general statement expressing the employer's dilemma : skilled craftsmen differ among themselves in respect to talent and training. He is therefore reluctant to allow the *fideiussor* to complete the job without the employer's consent. Ulpian is trying to preserve the employer's prerogative : he had contracted with a specific builder, presumably on the grounds that this builder possessed a certain level of skill. To allow the *fideiussor* to complete the job without the employer's approval robs him of his choice of a builder. The underlying assumption is that the *fideiussor* is not a specialist. To complete the contract, he would probably depend upon day labor or his own labor in order to reduce his costs. The employer would not be getting what he bargained for.

The interest of this text, beyond the evidence for the use of sureties, is in the jurist's concern for and recognition of the interests of parties to these

(42) Most scholars agree that the phrase *et hoc specialiter-perficiat* is a later interpolation. F. Eisele, *SZ* 18 (1897) 36 ; P. Bonfante, *Corso di diritto romano* VI (1930) 164 n. 1 ; T. Mayer-Maly, *LC* 100-101 ; S. Solazzi, *L'estinzione dell' obbligazione nel diritto romano* (1935) 39 ; on this text, see F. M. De Robertis, *I rapporti*, 38-39 and 163.

(43) See F. M. De Robertis, *I rapporti*, 163-164.

contracts. The employer has relied upon the skill of the builder and bargained for it. The builder, if he has defaulted, cannot escape the consequences of providing the employer with a remedy somewhat commensurate with the level of skill he had bound himself to provide.

As we can see, the texts on remedies and on securing the contract indicate that a cluster of agreements constituted the typical construction contract whether it was formed through *locatio* or through *stipulatio.* By the high classical period, *locatores* had become accustomed to including extra stipulations for penalties in case of delay, which would guarantee that a certain amount corresponding to his loss would be due in the event of a successful action on the stipulation. Parties to both types of contract made use of *fideiussio* to ensure that the builder's ability to finish the job or pay a pecuniary condemnation was guaranteed. The sureties would usually be bound to pay completion costs in the event of the builder's default. This move towards providing for a predictable outcome of a potential action may reflect the generalized interest in a more standardized form for construction contracts, perhaps the result of an increase in the volume of building activity in the early Empire.

CHAPTER IV

The Roman Jurists and Construction Practice in Rome

In the previous chapters, we have examined the network of rules developed over more than two centuries by the Roman jurists in response to the disputes presented to them by the parties to contracts for construction. This analysis concentrates upon the actual product of the legal system, that is, the juristic opinions which resolve individual cases, whether real or hypothetical, and have a normative effect upon the future legal behavior of builders and employers. There are, of course, serious limitations to the adequacy of the system which can be reconstructed from the surviving texts. Our picture is necessarily impaired by the condition of the legal texts themselves : as a result of post-classical epitomizing and Justinian's compilation, many sources have been lost, and the surviving texts lack much of the controversy which apparently characterized the jurists' discussions ([1]). Furthermore, none of these *Digest* texts can be linked to a specific historical case, and the lack of anything like court records or a literary treatment of a construction dispute means that the atmosphere of the forensic discussion is lost. Nevertheless, the texts present problems and solutions which are consistent with typical disputes in building and suggest important lines of discussion and controversy ([2]).

In this chapter, we will survey the accomplishment of juristic law in the area of construction. It seems clear from the analysis in the previous chapter that the duties and liabilities of each party to the contract underwent change during the period of classical jurisprudence as the jurists encountered cases

(1) On these limitations, see also B. W. Frier, *LTIR* 174-175. The consequences of the compilation for the condition of the texts are the subject of debate, M. Kaser, *Zur Methodologie der römischen Rechtsquellenforschung* in *SAWW* 277 (1972) and F. Wieacker, *SZ* 91 (1974) 1-40. On the role of controversy in juristic debate, A. A. Schiller, *Roman Law Mechanisms of Development* (1978) 284-291.

(2) See for example, M. S. Simon, *Construction Contracts and Claims* (1979), for typical legal pitfalls in modern construction contracts. Among the gaps in our knowledge of Roman practice is the precise role of the architect, although Vitruvius (1.1.10) gives some indication, see above at Chapter II, page 49 and note 23.

arising from difficult problems in construction. By analyzing the pattern of liabilities emerging from the texts, as well as the techniques used by the jurists in deciding cases, we will observe how they accomodated the competing demands of the parties and how the law evolved as a consequence. It may then be possible to speculate how changes and developments in the law related to growth in the building industry.

The Origins of Legal Claims in Construction

Before we proceed to examine the liabilities of builders and employers, it is important to consider how legal claims arose and what factors enabled building contractors to be successful in gaining access to the legal system. The demand for law does not arise from a vacuum, but often emerges from forces and interests in society. These forces, however, do not simply translate themselves into successful legal claims ; they are processed through legal culture, with the result that a number of screening factors weed out some claims while they transform others into actual demands for legal rules ([3]). Thus the law does not perfectly mirror society : "a person who understood the social structure of a society could not deduce the legal system from this structure" ([4]).

In order for a potential claimant to become a litigant, his grievance must be constituted and defined so as to permeate the barriers of substance, structure and legal culture. Structure involves the configuration of the system itself : can the court system accept and process the claim ? will it be convenient and possible to pursue a legal remedy ? Substance includes the actual legal rules ; before initiating an action, an individual might wish to consider whether the actual state of the law favors an acceptable outcome to his claim. Finally, there is legal culture, the "ideas, attitudes, beliefs, expectations, and opinions about the law" ([5]). Each of these three factors serves to aid the aggrieved party to get his claim to court, or to discourage him either by thwarting the claim or by handling it through an extra-legal method of dispute settlement.

(3) The following paragraphs rely upon the model of the legal system developed in L. Friedman, *The Legal System : A Social Science Perspective* (1975) 148-160 : "Social explanations of law then assume the existence of 'interests', which are converted into 'demands' and then produce responses in the legal system. It is the legal culture that presides over the conversion of interests into demands (150)". On the failings of social explanations of law emphasizing interests, see R. Gordon, *Stanford Law Review* 36 (1984) 72-73.

(4) L. Friedman (cited note 3), 149.

(5) On substance, structure and legal culture, see L. Friedman (cited note 3), 148-160.

Understanding the legal culture of any society is a difficult task, since it involves quantifying and describing complex and highly subjective attitudes and beliefs. Moreover, the accessibility of the legal system would not be viewed in the same way even by members of the same society, depending upon such factors as the individual's financial means and status in society. For Roman society the difficulties are exacerbated by the lack of any quantity of evidence documenting daily life in the Roman courts ([6]). There is also no true consensus concerning which groups in society Roman law particularly served. It has often been maintained that much of Roman law was principally designed for the use of the upper classes, and certain areas of the law demonstrate this assertion. However, it is also increasingly being recognized that Roman law, and in particular contract law, was developed in close relationship to the interests of a more broadly defined commercially oriented class ([7]).

The results of this study appear to confirm an awareness, at least on the part of the jurists, of the particular problems associated with building and building contractors. The relative accessibility of the legal system to contractors is attributable to many factors relating to the receptivity of the system to claims and the capacity of the claimants to formulate and press demands. Contract law is well developed in Roman law and had a long history in public and in private construction. Conversely, other ways of employing builders, although little understood, as we have seen in Chapter II, may not have been conducive to the generation of lawsuits, and may instead have favored other methods of settlement. The combined screens of substance, structure and legal culture would have prevented many grievances from being considered as possible bases for legal action. Slave builders and freed builders working for their patrons may have constituted a large part of the skilled labor force and probably participated in sizeable projects within the *familia*, under the supervision of master, patron or another builder ([8]).

(6) Certain aspects of Roman legal culture are studied in J. M. Kelly, *Studies in the Civil Judicature of the Roman Republic* (1976), especially chapter four ; *Roman Litigation* (1966) chapter three ; P. Garnsey, *Social Status and Legal Privilege in the Roman Empire* (1970).

(7) On the utility of Roman law for the upper classes, D. Daube, *Roman Law, Linguistic, Social and Philosophical Aspects* (1969) 65-128. On the incorporation of usages in the wine trade into the juristic law, see B. W. Frier, *SZ* 100 (1983) 257-295. G. Rickman, *Roman Granaries and Store Buildings* (1971) 194-204, demonstrates the importance of the connection between the law and its economic context. It is unlikely that all areas of Roman law can be explained solely in regard to the demands of any single group.

(8) In general, slaves could not bring claims in court. On legal aspects of Roman slavery,

For these builders, there were deterrents to the use of the legal system : in addition to the formal barriers imposed by law, low status and the dependence of the builder upon the employer discouraged legal claims. Builders hired on contracts for day labor may well have brought actions against employers, who were sometimes other builders, but there is no evidence of what they did. These suits would have been for the value of individual days of work ([9]).

Contracting created a negotiated, arms-length relationship, based upon mutual bargaining between two individuals. For the purposes of the contract, they agreed and were bound in a relationship of relative equality and may have had no other form of social contact. This would have increased the likelihood that disputes were settled in litigation ([10]). Moreover, contractors may have been the only builders to negotiate and carry out private jobs of a size sufficient to make an action worthwhile in terms of potential financial gain or loss. It seems from the legal texts that builders of fairly large projects, such as *insulae*, villas and houses, used the legal system ; they had the capacity to organize materials and labor and to secure the necessary *fideiussores* ([11]). In entering into a contract, the builder was wagering on his ability to finish the work and earn a profit within the bounds of the negotiated price. If his wager turned out to be unfavorable, he may have been willing to risk an action in court because of the size of his potential loss.

see W. W. BUCKLAND, *The Roman Law of Slavery* (1908). A slave with *peculium* had a broader range of possibilities, see above Chapter III, section D, on Nicephorus, the (presumably) servile *uilicus* of Cicero's brother Quintus (CIC. *Q.Fr.* 3.1.5). On the duties of freedmen to their patrons, M. KASER, *RPR*[2] I 298-301. Many freed builders appear to have worked independently as contractors (see above Chapter II).

(9) On contracts for day labor, *locatio conductio operarum*, see M. KASER, *RPR*[2] I 568-570. The size of the contracts, as in the one implied in D.19.2.30.3, see above at Chapter III, section D, was probably relatively small.

(10) D. BLACK, *The Behavior of Law* (1976), especially chapters one and two on stratification and morphology, asserts that differentiations in status and social distance can predict how much access people will have to law.

(11) Little is known about the costs of such structures. Cicero's houses at Tusculum and Formiae were worth HS 500,000 and HS 250,000 respectively, but these figures represent the value of both land and structure, not building costs (*Att.* 4.2.5). See R. DUNCAN-JONES, *PBSR* 33 (1965) 177-188, on the property of the younger Pliny ; Pliny mentions a temple he has promised to Tifernum Tiberinum, but gives no cost (10.8.2-4). The building costs recorded in DUNCAN-JONES, *The Economy of the Roman Empire*[2] (1982) 157-162, are illustrative. It seems likely that in the Empire the largest projects were public works which would have been administered by the state, see above Chapter II, pages 60-62 and notes 73-80.

The Parties' Claims in *Locatio-Condvctio*

The employer's claims against the builder in an *actio locati* reflect four broad areas of interest which develop from his primary concern, the acquisition of a finished structure on his property ([12]).

A. In hiring the builder as a professional, the employer seeks to obtain the skilled and accurate performance of the job. Through *probatio,* he ascertains that both of these requirements have been fulfilled. This process involved comparing the actual building to the specifications which formed part of the initial agreement. The specifications were probably based upon an architect's plan. The parties could agree to alter some of the provisions in the contract after the formation, and Labeo allowed a subsequent, apparently verbal, change in the specifications to supersede a term in the original contract (D.19.2.60.3).

The right to approve the work was a powerful exercise of the employer's interest in skilled completion. According to Javolenus, it sufficed that the employer had concluded the contract with the intention of approving the work at the end : he was not required to include a specific clause naming the approver or requesting an approval. The right to conduct an approval was implied in the contract of *locatio operis* (D.19.2.51.1). There were, however, limitations placed upon the approval process. In general, the jurists assume that a successful *probatio* marked the end of the builder's liability for the work (Labeo, D.19.2.62 ; Florentinus, D.19.2.36). The employer was discouraged from delaying in conducting approval (D.19.2.36). Paul, perhaps summarizing earlier developments, precluded the possibility of an action on the contract after approval unless the employer could establish that the builder had acted fraudulently in obtaining the approval (D.19.2.24 pr.). Finally, the employer's evaluation of the quality of the structure had to conform to the judgment of a 'good man', a development to which we will return below (D.19.2.24 pr.).

B. Another related aspect of the employer's reliance upon the skill of the builder was his desire to assign to him overall risk for the construction

(12) The interpretations in the following pages are derived from the analysis of the sources presented in Chapter III, sections A-E. On the function of interests and their role in the formulation of claims, see above at note 3 and J. Stone, *The Social Dimensions of Law and Justice* (1966) 164-198 ; B. W. Frier, *LTIR* 174-219 ; A. A. Schiller, *Columbia Law Review* 58 (1958) 1226-1238. Cf. A. Watson, *Society and Legal Change* (1977).

project during the contract period. The builder was clearly responsible for the execution of the construction, but his responsibility for the building site itself was an area of controversy. The employer furnished the site, and his retention of ownership is explicitly mentioned as a distinguishing trait of *locatio* (Pomponius and Sabinus, D.18.1.20 ; Paul, D.19.2.22.1-2 ; Ulpian, D.6.1.39). But the employer was reluctant to assume the risk if the building sustained any damage during construction as a result of the collapse or subsidence of the building site. Labeo seems to have upheld the employer's interest in attributing to the builder a broad, undifferentiated risk for the site (D.19.2.62). Beginning with Sabinus, however, in D.19.2.59, the employer was responsible for destruction caused by *uis naturalis*. This opinion quickly became a feature of subsequent opinions (Florentinus, D.19.2.36 ; Javolenus, D.19.2.37). The employer's area of control was substantially broadened by Paul in D.19.2.62 to include *uitium soli*, which comprised not only responsibility for natural disasters, such as earthquake, but also for weakness in the soil. Therefore, by the end of the classical period of jurisprudence the employer could not expect to transfer complete risk for the project to the builder.

C. The employer was especially concerned with ensuring timely completion of the job or, at the very least, attempting to mitigate the consequences of delay. This problem receives a great deal of attention in the surviving texts on construction, and employers were probably persistent in seeking actions before the end of the contract term in cases where delay was manifest. In general, the jurists were disinclined to grant an action before the end of the fixed term, and this rule applied both to the action on the contract and on any ancillary agreements or clauses whose fulfillment depended upon the builder's default (Ulpian, D.19.2.13.10 ; 45.1.72.1). The employer's most effective recourse was to wait and try to obtain the completion costs or other remedies as soon as the date had passed (Ulpian, D.45.1.72.1 ; 19.2.13.10 ; Javolenus, D.46.1.44).

As a way of mitigating the loss in time and money which often arose as a result of the builder's default, the employer could omit a fixed term from the clauses, in the hope that a plea of delay (with some evidence) would be sufficient to allow an earlier action. It is hard to judge how successful this tactic was in practice. Labeo instructed that the appropriate date for an action would fall due after the lapse of a period of time deemed adequate for the construction project in the judgment of a 'good man' (D.19.2.58.1). This technique, the use of the *arbitrium boni uiri*, appears first in reference to a contract of *locatio conductio,* but also figures in the texts on stipulation, as we will see below. An explicit completion date was not subject to reevaluation through the application of the *arbitrium boni uiri* (Paul, D.19.2.24 pr.).

D. The employer generally depended upon the builder or an architect to formulate the contract price, the *pretium certum,* which represented his financial obligation to the builder. In practice, employers were evidently accustomed to small increases in building costs and probably agreed to pay them in the interest of completing the contract. But the *locator* would have to agree to any extra payment above the contract price, and in one case, the employer refused to approve a 50% increase in cost. Labeo allowed him to terminate the contract (D.19.2.60.4).

The builder's primary goal in the contract was to earn his living through the exercise of his skill. He hoped to emerge at the end of the contract with the work complete and his *merces* in full, having incurred no unnecessary expenses along the way. In *locatio,* his interest lay in combating the employer's attempts to hold him responsible for any extra expenses arising during the project, and his claims sought full payment (or a *pro rata* portion) against the employer's charges of faulty work, delay or damage.

A'. Several sources emphasize that the builder's primary contribution to the contract is his expertise as a skilled worker. His job involves the improvement of the property which is entrusted to him by the employer. This is the essential characteristic of *locatio conductio operis* as a contract, and the means whereby it is differentiated from *emptio uenditio.* In general, the artisan has no property interest in the material he works on, which is the employer's property transferred into the builder's control for the term of the job (Papinian and Sabinus, D.18.1.20 ; Paul, D.19.2.22.1-2). Along the same lines, the builder's financial interest in the building materials is strictly limited. He doesn't always furnish them, although he may typically supply the most common elements used for walling. In any case, they are not his property and his job only involves transforming them into a finished product (Ulpian, D.6.1.39 ; Paul, citing Labeo, D.50.16.5.1).

B'. The builder's responsibility for risk for the entire project during the contract period undergoes a gradual differentiation from the rather broad, early conception implied by Labeo in D.19.2.62. Subsequent jurisprudence erodes this broad sphere of control (Sabinus, D.19.2.59 ; Florentinus, 19.2.36 ; see above at B). Paul defines the builder's responsibility as comprising *uitium operis,* excluding any risk for damage to the building site, whether owing to earthquake or inherent defects. The builder's liability for the job is narrowed to include only those aspects directly pertaining to skill and quality. This is not made explicit, as it is in other areas of *locatio conductio*, by creating a liability for *imperitia*, but is determined through the mechanism of *probatio*, perhaps because it had long been a feature of these contracts.

C'. The builder had a strong interest in obtaining the full contract period for his job, and the jurists' tendency to uphold the fixed date surely worked in his favor most of the time. Even in the absence of a fixed time limit, he could rely upon a 'reasonable time' to finish his work before the employer could bring an action (Javolenus and Labeo, D.19.2.58.1). Furthermore, if he did delay, he was not responsible for paying any damages or penalties if the employer did not follow his own provisions exactly (Ulpian, D.19.2.13.10). The sureties received the same protection (Javolenus, D.46.1.44).

D'. General practice established that the builder usually received half of his payment at the beginning of the job and the other half after completion and approval. The builder probably tried to avoid using his own resources to complete the project, but the portion he received at the beginning could not have taken him very far. A great deal depended upon the number of workers he hired and whether or not he was supplying the materials. Although in general full payment came after approval, the builder could, under certain circumstances, obtain partial payment in mid-term, as in the particular case when he wished to pay a stoneworker who had completed a portion of the work (Alfenus/Servius, D.19.2.30.3).

The Parties' Claims in *Stipvlatio*

The contract of *stipulatio* provided an executory agreement to perform an activity embodied in a briefly formulated promise, presumably accompanied by specifications. The basic interests of the parties are the same, but the choice of *stipulatio* frees them from many of the implied duties involved in *locatio conductio*. Much of the interpretation focuses upon the development of general principles in the law of *stipulatio*, such as rules for the formation of a valid contract, the interpretation of the words of the promise, and the problems of promises 'to do' (*facere*).

a. The promise was invalid if the construction site was not named, reflecting the employer's basic goal, the improvement of his property

(Papinian, D.45.1.115 pr. ; Ulpian, 13.4.2.5). In some cases, the jurists were willing to enforce a contract lacking this explicit term if other evidence of the employer's interest in construction on this site could be adduced. Marcellus considered valid a *stipulatio* for the construction of an *insula* even when the promise lacked explicit reference to the building site, so long as the location was apparent and the employer's interest in the job could be demonstrated (D.45.1.95).

b. Most of the sources on stipulations for construction involve the employer's provisions for timely completion. The general notion that a fixed time limit must be observed, even if the builder has done no work, is maintained in *stipulatio* (Papinian, D.45.1.124). As in *locatio*, there is the possibility of leaving a gap in the agreement and allowing the problem of delay to be worked out in a subsequent action if necessary (Pomponius, citing Celsus, D.45.1.14). According to Venuleius (D.45.1.137.2-3), the employer must wait until the 'adequate time' has elapsed according to the judgment of a good man. The issue of delay and timely completion put an obstacle in the way of employers who would have preferred to sue as soon as delay became apparent ; they were often forced to abide by their own explicit terms or made to rely upon the good faith of the builder in waiting out the implied 'reasonable time'.

In practice, some of the employer's arguments may have been convincing. Why should he wait to bring an action if 75% of the term has elapsed and no work has been done, or, the more compelling example, he has contracted for a builder to prop up a collapsing apartment, and the builder is delaying ? Ulpian was in favor of granting an early action in both instances, and there are hints that other jurists endorsed bringing an early end to the contract in favor of the employer's interest in diminishing the potential for loss through delay (Marcellus, D.45.1.98.1 ; Ulpian, D.45.1.72.2).

The builder's interests in a contract in stipulation are less accessible through the texts than they are in *locatio*, and correspond to those outlined above for the employer.

a'. The major area of conflict is the builder's delay, and the jurists are willing in most cases to enforce the full time limit, or infer an adequate one, so that he will not be threatened by an early action. The jurists develop the notion of the adequate time required for the task as an inherent part of the job (D.45.1.73 pr.) and use the same technique in texts on ancillary stipulations or stipulations providing *fideiussores* (D.45.1.14 ; 45.1.72.1).

Venuleius (D.45.1.137.2-3) infers the idea of a 'natural' time for the obligation, namely the time within which a 'diligent builder' would have completed the job. He justifies this on the grounds that the builder should not be hurried in his work, presumably because haste leads to poor building practice.

b'. As we have seen, the builder could not escape liability for finishing the job by arguing that the destruction had been caused by *uis maior.* Therefore, when his work is destroyed by fire, the best he can hope for is the full contract term again to complete the work (Pomponius, D.45.1.15). Since there is no generalized discussion of risk in the texts on *stipulatio,* this opinion is not necessarily to be considered broadly applicable. The builder would still have to cover the expenses of finishing the building.

In sharp contradistinction to *locatio conductio, stipulatio* appears to lack any built-in mechanism for approval. It is clear that the goal of stipulating for a builder's services is the same as in *locatio*: the employer intends to engage a skilled builder who will take charge of the project (implied in D.46.3.31). But *stipulatio* existed as an alternative method of employment with a different pattern of duties and obligations. The interpretation of the builder's obligation did not allow for such mitigating factors as *uis maior,* as we have seen, nor was the quality of the work evaluated according to the *arbitrium boni uiri.* Only in regard to delay was the notion of good faith introduced, stemming from the notion that obligations 'to do' implied a period of time necessary for their fulfillment. Good faith considerations do not seem to have been introduced in regard to other aspects of the builder's obligation which was probably judged strictly according to whether or not he had performed on time. The jurists never allude to any approval process. Indeed, the evaluation of quality in contracts in *stipulatio* is never mentioned, but it seems likely that the employer's interest in supervising the careful execution of the terms was increased. Many employers may have preferred to contract through *stipulatio* precisely because it did not require that the standard of good faith be introduced into the evaluation of the parties' behavior ([13]).

(13) *Stipulatio* may have been particularly well suited to contracts for the construction of *insulae* if anything can be inferred from the contents of the juristic texts (see above at Chapter I, n. 29). The characteristics of the obligation created by *stipulatio* may have been more suited to a relatively standardized structure destined for commercial use.

THE JURISTS' LAW AND RELATIONS WITH THE CONSTRUCTION INDUSTRY

As we have seen, the formation and execution of the contract, as well as its adjudication in an action, bring together two distinct sets of interests united temporarily for the accomplishment of a particular goal. In responding to legal questions, the jurists evaluate the behavior and performance of the parties against the terms of their agreement and often choose to interpret the activities of the parties strictly according to the terms. One important principle underlying the contract system in general was a belief that contracts should be enforced and held sacred by the law. This view of contractual obligations tends to support a system in which the property owner's right to exploit or improve his property is considered absolute ([14]). The parties, at least for the purpose of the obligation, are treated as equals who have negotiated their terms, and once they have arrived at the agreement, they can generally count upon the law to maintain its security. The jurists rarely interfere in the terms of the agreement. It is more common to find the jurists enforcing the clauses even to the detriment of the party who agreed to them.

The texts on the builder's delay illustrate this tendency clearly : the employer observes that the builder will not finish the structure by the deadline fixed in the contract. He wishes to bring an action. In general, in the texts as they have survived, the jurists enforce the contract term as the appropriate date for bringing an action and will not allow an early action (Papinian, D.45.1.124). This practice may have in turn encouraged the parties to omit the completion date. Another example occurs in the text on the duties of sureties. Javolenus (D.46.1.44) forbids an employer from holding a *fideiussor* liable for completion costs because the employer has failed to find a second *locator*. According to the terms of the stipulation, the sureties were responsible for the price of a new contract of *locatio*. When this contract did not materialize, the jurist found that the employer had not fulfilled his part of the promise ([15]).

Circumstances, however, often transform the contract into a hard bargain, with the result that the parties prefer either to escape the agreement alto-

(14) F. SCHULZ, *Principles of Roman Law* (1936) 225-227, attributes this quality of contract law to the concept of *fides*. Cf. ULPIAN (32 *ad ed.*), D.19.1.11.1. On the role of the legal system in protecting the right to use and disposition of private property, see CICERO, *Off.* 1.23 ; 2.78, and M. W. FREDERIKSEN, *JRS* 65 (1966) 128-141 ; B. W. FRIER, *RRJ* 184-188. On the modern concept of freedom of contract, see P. S. ATIYAH, *The Rise and Fall of Freedom of Contract* (1979), on which see B. MENSCH, *Stanford Law Review* 33 (1981) 753-772.

(15) See the discussion above at pages 133-134.

gether or to renegotiate the terms. For example, in D.19.2.60.4, the contract price is found to be insufficient by 50% ; the builder evidently stops work and seeks to secure a promise of 50% more than the original contract price before he will resume his work. In this instance, the interference of the jurists in the security of the contract is actively sought as a remedy to the situation. Labeo grants the employer the right to end the contract ([16]).

In many cases, the legal issues are not able to be resolved by examining the terms of the contract, and the jurists must consider the broader issues underlying the liability of each party. As a result, the duties and obligations of the parties became increasingly differentiated and defined during the classical period of jurisprudence in such a way as to effect a significant alteration in their liabilities. One example occurs in regard to unanticipated loss or damage to the building or the site. Events such as landslide or subsidence of the earth render the terms of the contract costly and difficult to perform. The parties seek some solution other than strict enforcement of the contract terms. Paul appears to use the principle of spheres of control as a way of apportioning the risk for damage : the builder is responsible for faults in the work and the employer assumes risk for the site (D.19.2.62). This narrows the builder's liabilities by exempting him from risk for damage caused by weakness in the building site ([17]).

Another important principle in the development of jurists' law in construction is the *arbitrium boni uiri* and its use in mediating between the subjective viewpoints of the parties. This technique is used primarily in *locatio* in regard to evaluating the builder's performance. In D.19.2.24 pr., Paul states that the *qualitas* of the work, comprising both skill and conformity, can only be measured by comparison with the level of quality a 'good man' would find reasonable. This technique mitigates against the application of the subjective evaluation of the employer, and asserts the utility of a standard based upon what is commonly held to be sufficient ([18]).

The *arbitirium boni uiri* is also introduced as a technique for determining the 'reasonable' completion date in contracts in both *locatio* and *stipulatio* when a fixed term is lacking. Labeo (D.19.2.58.1) develops the use of this method from his idea of the 'intentions' of the parties to a good faith contract. Venuleius (D.45.1.137.3) calls for the use of the 'good man' in evaluating obligations in *stipulatio*, normally not governed by a good faith

(16) See the discussion above at pages 117-120. See also D.19.2.13.10.
(17) See the discussion above at pages 90-92.
(18) Cf. ULPIAN, D.21.1.19.4, and the discussion above at pages 109-113.

standard, and provides a detailed model for conducting the necessary investigations into standard practices ([19]). Such detail is absent from the texts on *locatio*, but the use of the technique itself implies recourse to generally held norms defining a reasonably good builder. Of course, the use of the good man standard was not universally accepted, particularly in the law on *stipulatio*. Ulpian asserts the importance of another obvious consideration which could outweigh the importance of the 'reasonable time' rule : the employer's interest in having the structure completed to a deadline (D.45.1.72.2). It seems likely that this conflict arose frequently and was a subject of controversy during the classical period.

The use of a 'good man' standard led to a diminution in the importance of the employer's subjective vision of the finished product, and encouraged a professionally-oriented standard of what was acceptable. The jurists eroded the prerogatives of the individual employer so as to place the builder on a more predictable and less risky footing in entering into a contract. Moreover, the use of a good faith technique, such as the standard of a 'good man', encouraged the evaluation of the individual performance of the builder in accordance with the demands of the contract and the general practices in the trade. It seems safe to assume that information about standard building practices was available to the *iudex*. The jurists appear to have adopted this method of resolving claims as particularly well suited to the problems of building, and they tried to strike a balance between the employer, lacking in skill, but with a financial and property interest, and the builder, a skilled craftsman. This willingness to consult practices prevalent in commercial practice as a source of standards and of law is characteristic of the jurists and is attested in other areas of the law ([20]).

As we can see, there was an evolution in the legal treatment of claims brought by builders and their employers during the period of classical Roman jurisprudence which effectuated a narrowing of the builder's liabilities in the areas of risk, level of quality and speed of completion. This mirrors the development we have seen in regard to the builder's overall responsibility for the job and the construction site during the contract period. Although the reasons for change in the law are always difficult to describe or trace

(19) See the discussion above at pages 83-84.

(20) On the *arbitrium boni uiri*, see P. Voci, *Le obbligazioni romane* I i (1969) 190-204 ; F. Gallo, *Studi in onore di G. Grosso* III (1970) 534-540. On the function of 'reasonableness' as a way to introduce larger social interests into contractual relations, see J. Stone (cited note 12), 196-198. On the influence of commercial practice on the law, see above at note 7.

accurately, it does at least seem likely that the impetus to change arose from the immediate context of the Roman building trade and that the jurists were influenced in a number of ways by the growth and transformation of the building industry ([21]).

As we have seen in Chapter II, the period of the first 150 years of the Empire witnessed a rapid growth in many types of construction from public works to monuments to private housing. The rise and growth of the *collegium* of the *fabri tignarii* in Rome and in Ostia indicate that builders were increasingly identified as a group with a distinct professional identity. It is probably not unreasonable to assume that the professional interests of the trade at large became articulated as building activity increased and legal issues in construction received more attention. As cases reached the jurists, the concerns of builders, and specifically contractors, would increasingly be put before the legal system and the system adapted to the needs of these specialized claimants.

In general, as has been suggested, the jurists rely upon a strategy whereby the parties bargain for the contract they desire with the expectation that the jurists will refrain from interfering in the content of the agreement. But the jurists are willing to incorporate the use of prevailing standards in the trade to evaluate the contractor's work, a trend which diminishes the importance of the employer's assessment of the quality of the construction. The effect of these developments, of course, can only be the subject of speculation. Ideally, the building trade was probably encouraged by the trends in the jurisprudence to promote a generalized level of skill and quality which could be broadly construed as adequate. This standard would raise the lowest levels of construction practice to an acceptable level. Thus the increased sense of professionalism and predictability which came to characterize legal relations between builders and employers may have, in turn, fostered better building pratices.

(21) On the role of social forces in initiating changes in the law, see L. Friedman (cited note 3), 269-309.

INDEX OF SOURCES

I. Legal Sources

II. Literary Sources

III. Inscriptions

GENERAL INDEX

TABLE OF CONTENTS